Mrs. Richard Landorf is "Joyce" to thousands. Her confidence in the Lord Jesus Christ and her wit are a winning combination to put listeners and readers at ease. She has made three record albums and written more than a dozen books, including *The Fragrance of Beauty* (Victor). She is the mother of a son, Rick, and a daughter, Laurie, both married. Joyce and her husband, Dick, live in Rancho Mirage, California.

"Joyce, I Feel Like I Know You"

Based on letters and conversations
about life's pressure points.
JOYCE LANDORF

While this book is designed for the reader's personal use and profit, it is also intended for group study. A leader's guide is available from your local bookstore or from the publisher.

VICTOR BOOKS

a division of SP Publications, Inc.
WHEATON ILLINOIS 60187

Offices also in Fullerton, California • Whitby, Ontario, Canada • Amersham-on-the-Hill, Bucks, England

Eighth printing, 1982

Library of Congress Catalog Card Number:

ISBN: 0–88207–742–2

VICTOR BOOKS
A division of SP Publications, Inc.
P.O. Box 1825 • Wheaton, Ill. 60187

Contents

A word from Joyce . . .

This book would not have been possible without the many people who were willing to share their concerns, their fears, and their successes with me. My thanks to all of you who have so unselfishly contributed to this work.

Once again I must thank Brenda Arnold and Sheila Rapp for their loving help with spelling, editing, and professional typing. They are very special and deserve a lion's share of credit for every book I write.

Last, but not in the least, I thank Jim Adair and the entire staff of Victor Books at Scripture Press for working very hard to bring mere words into real books!

Thank you, one and all.

1

Is Total Honesty
Always the Best Policy?

Joyce, I hope it's all right to call you Joyce.

Yes, of course! Everyone does.

I suppose I should address you as Mrs. Landorf, but when I read your books and hear you speak, you seem to be talking just to me. So I feel like I know you.

In a real way you *do*. And even though I hear the phrase "I feel like I know you" seemingly every time I turn around, it still makes my day! When the door of writing was opened to me, I felt a tremendous responsibility to reveal real, live experiences with loving, yet candid, honesty. So you *do* know me, even though our friendship is through the pages of a book, and a little one-sided since I can't get your feedback or have a back-and-forth conversation.

It's probably because of your honesty that I really identify with you. Does writing in such a way come easily for you?

No, it's never easy to be completely honest. There are at least two problems! (1) Being honest leaves us wide open and vulnerable to reactions or criticisms and, (2) being honest *can* be destructive and annihilate another person's self-esteem and character if it's not handled carefully. So while I don't feel it's difficult to be honest, I *do* feel the risk of being honest.

How then do you work around these two problems?

The way porcupines make love—very carefully! Joe Bayly, writer and publishing executive, was an enormous help to me the first time I met him. We were at an autographing party together. I had just written *Let's Have a Banquet or Will $1.36 Be Enough?* (Zondervan) and was in the middle of my manuscript for *His Stubborn Love* (also Zondervan). As writers will, Joe asked me how the work was going. (I thought he'd never ask.) I told him I wanted to write honestly, but since much of my life before Christ had been ugly, I was reluctant to write about it. I was even having a hard time remembering those tragic years. I asked him directly, "Joe, some of the material concerning my past is too painful to write down. I'm not convinced it would do any good anyway, so how can I be honest about that period of my life?"

His answer became my guideline for honest writing. He said, "The question is not, 'How can I be honest?' but 'How much should I reveal?' Prayerfully decide what parts of your past God wants you to reveal and then write honestly."

You said being honest leaves us vulnerable to people's reactions. Has that been a problem in your writing?

Yes, once or twice. For instance, I honestly felt God wanted me to share some distasteful incidents in a couple of my books—so I wrote about them as I had seen them. However, some members of my family were not too thrilled with my sharing what they felt was personal—particularly since the experiences were not victorious, happy, or successful.

We all wear masks, and most of us want to be presented in the best possible way at all times. For instance, when I write a true story that isn't complimentary, the people involved try to explain away their actions. I can't blame them for defending themselves, but there are difficult conflicts that DO happen. To say they don't happen—or didn't happen—is lying.

Yet I feel there is a need for Christian writers to tell things as they are—not just as they wish them to be. Don't you think that some books are written in a fantasy version where discouragement, failure, and fatigue are things that never happen to a real, born-again saint?

Yes, and I couldn't agree with you more. In many biographical and autobiographical accounts of Christians' lives, we have all read things like, "Those days were hard and we were discouraged, but God brought us through. The next day we went down the river and ministered to a new tribe." And we've all wondered, "How did you get from 'discouragement' to 'ministering' without passing 'Go' and collecting your two hundred dollars?" After we read accounts like that, we are filled with a sense of guilt because we don't seem to be made of the same stuff as other Christians, and we inadvertently form unrealistic comparisons between them and ourselves.

One of the great things about the writers of the Old and New Testaments is that, in honesty, they wrote the whole truth. King David, the psalmist, had his dark side (adultery and murder, to name two), yet it was recorded along with all the good he did. I'm glad the Bible was written that way. Humanly speaking, I'm sure David would not have been pleased to have all the garbage of his life presented, yet I'm glad David's weaknesses were told, because they give me hope when I've sinned or made mistakes. In one story after another, God shows first the human weaknesses and failures of His people and then His mighty power, control, and His loving, forgiving plan. What a God we serve!

Earlier you said honesty causes two problems (vulnerability and destruction) and you shared that some of your own family were not too happy about your honesty. Are you hinting that honesty—at least sometimes—is not the best policy?

I suppose in a way I am, because there needs to be a warning sounded about honesty. Remember, I said, "I felt a tremendous responsibility to reveal real, live experiences with loving, yet candid, honesty." The two key words here are "responsibility" and "loving. Honesty, when NOT framed by responsibility and love, is atheistic and horribly cruel.

Our whole society has gone ape over the total-honesty concept. This concept is being preached from every pinnacle around. The hue and cry seems to be, "By all means, no matter what the cost or hurt (to you or others), let everything hang out—honestly." In fact, each decade brings a new psychological fad into prominence, and marriage counselors, psychologists, and psychiatrists jump on the bandwagon. This is the decade of honestly showing (and verbalizing) ALL your feelings. The reasoning behind verbal exposure seems to be that we have submerged our real feelings for 200 years, and now it's time to open up. We have never been mad and screamed at the boss or cried when we hurt (especially men); instead we have kept a tight, rigid hold on our inner emotions. This behavior is so bad, they say, that now we are being asked to do a complete turnabout. Instead of controlling our emotions or hiding them, we are encouraged to let everything hang out—and hang out honestly, by all means. However, as I've said, the down-to-earth problems are that it is not easy to be honest, and that honesty brings complications. Besides that, the total-honesty concept is certainly not a scriptural concept.

Then what attitude should I have toward honesty, especially when I am angry, unhappy, or emotionally upset?

I feel it should be smack in the middle between letting everything hang out and keeping all feelings hidden.

Can you give me a "for instance"?

Yes. It was Keith Miller who first talked about two kinds of honesty: *loving* or *atheistic*. I see these two distinct kinds practiced every day.

Let's say you see your friend across the room in your Sunday School class. She looks absolutely ghastly. She has big blue circles under her eyes, her hair is a disaster area, and she is as much fun as a Mafia funeral. If you are into the total-honesty concept, you walk over to her, and—with utter honesty, sincerity, and no malice aforethought— you say, "You look like death warmed over!" What you have said is honest, all right, but you have just shot down the last of an already dwindling supply of self-esteem. You have assassinated a human being's worth with your remark in a display of *atheistic* honesty. There is no love in honesty like that. It is not just a suggestion that we Christians do everything in love; it is a high command.

A woman I know prides herself on always letting everything hang out—honestly. She speaks what she feels, freely and fearlessly. The same woman wonders aloud but privately to me about her lack of friends and her inability to keep a friend once she gets one. She is the first to say, "Nobody likes me." Her deep-seated loneliness stems from the fact that she practices an honest approach daily, without loving responsibility.

Atheistic honesty is one thing; loving honesty, quite another. (The two are a world apart in the way they are demonstrated and the reactions they produce.)

Let's go back to the woman in the Sunday School class who looks so bad. Loving honesty says gently, "Hi, Hon. How are things going lately?"

Because this query brings no threat of any kind, the woman can honestly share and communicate with you.

Her haggard look is completely within reason when she explains she's been up all night with a sick child. Her look of exhaustion is completely understandable as she blurts out that she's just found out her husband is having an affair with his secretary. Or she's let her hair get a mess because she's found a small but definite lump on her breast, and she couldn't care less about her hair. Or maybe her look of fatigue is not about one of these ultra-serious things, but she's just weary of "well-doing, daily" routine. Whatever her reasons, had you told her honestly how she looked she would have never communicated her real inner workings to you. In fact your "honesty" would have done nothing to help her, and your "truth" would have opened up an old (or new) wound.

The loving question of "How's it going?" gives the other person the permission to verbalize and really share her feelings. It also says you're listening, and most of us desperately want—at some point in our lives—someone to listen. A woman I've never met writes in her long letter to me, "I guess the main reason for this letter is that I need to find someone to listen to me—someone who knows how I feel inside."

Are you saying, then, that as Christians we should never speak in a direct, honest way which may offend?

No, absolutely not. But you'd better be sure the Holy Spirit is guiding the words. I notice when Paul was unhappy with the conduct or the spiritual progress of his congregations, his letters begin with love and end with honest responsibility. He told them lovingly and truthfully where they were failing and how to shape up, but he always spoke with the wisdom and love of the Holy Spirit's guidance.

It is no secret that my mother was very outspoken, but she always felt a keen responsibility to loving honesty, and opposed atheistic honesty with all her heart. She was an articulate Hungarian woman, but her deepest desire was to use her speaking ability for God's glory. I know because she and I prayed many times about OUR mouths and what came out of them. She saw early in my Christian life that being outspoken was one of my inherited traits and, while she wanted me to remain outspoken, she wanted me to seek the Holy Spirit's wisdom whenever I spoke out.

I remember a critical, verbal woman in my father's church. I remember her particularly well because her sharp tongue was often aimed at my mother as the "pastor's wife." Even when cancer began to eat away at Mother, the woman kept up her dismal commentary. Of course, she never said these things directly and never discussed her conflicts with Mother—only with others.

My mother was unable to attend church regularly as cancer advanced, but one Sunday she did go and ran smack into this very woman. Those who saw the meeting said there was a rather depressed expression on Mother's face when the woman threw her arms around her and exclaimed, "Oh, Marion! It's so good to see you here at church again!" Her greeting was something of a news bulletin, and my mother sensed instantly the woman did not mean a word of what she said. If Mother was depressed at her greeting, she was downright nauseated when the woman ended her remarks by giving her a re-sounding kiss on the cheek.

I'm not sure whether or not my mother checked out her next words with the Holy Spirit, but I rather think she did because with no bitterness or meanness in her voice whatsoever, she took one little step backward, looked the woman in the eye, and said clearly, "That was a Judas kiss and I don't want you ever to do that again."

My mother felt betrayed by this woman, and I'm still amazed at her loving, responsible honesty when she called the kiss exactly what it was.

The woman never had an opportunity to kiss her again, for Mother died less than two months later.

The "truth" in this case did hurt, but my mother met the confrontation with loving honesty. So there is a time to speak out and have a conflict aired or cleared, but only with the Holy Spirit's wisdom and the "loving honesty" Paul displayed.

Earlier you said the total-honesty concept is not a spiritual concept. Does the Bible really back up the loving-honesty theory?

Unmistakably, and in many places. Here are just a few examples.

The epistles 1, 2, and 3 John present loving honesty, the need for it, and the ways to accomplish it. They are short, easy-to-read books, wedged in between Peter and Jude. I suggest you read one of the new translations or paraphrased editions, which are remarkably clear. As you read these books, it's important to remember they were written to Christians—not unbelievers. So as early as the First Century, Christians were having problems with honesty and how to handle it.

Then in Ephesians, chapter 4, we read that we are to forbear one another in love (v. 2), to speak the truth in love (v. 15), and to edify each other in love (v. 16). This is only one chapter from the Bible, but the guidelines for honesty are clearly defined as love and loving behavior.

In Colossians 2:2 we are encouraged to be "knit together in love," and 1 Thessalonians 5:13 tells us to "esteem them very highly in love." How beautiful of our Lord to want us to be truthful and to give us the key to honesty—the Jesus-type of love.

We show this love when our living, listening, walking, and especially speaking are done in His love. Only then can we be truly honest with others.

Loving honesty will not annihilate another human's feelings of self-worth, but will promote reconciliation, resolve conflicts, and heal emotions.

Isn't it interesting when we go back to God's Word and obey His instructions? We see that He has already made a way for us to be honest. Really lovingly honest!

2

Friendship—
The Two-Way-Street
Relationship

We all know that in order to have a friend we have to be one first. In your busy schedule between writing, speaking, traveling and being a wife and mother, how difficult it is to be a friend?

Very.

My husband and I have often joked about how lousy our social life has become. In fact, it's practically nonexistent. Well, that's not *exactly* true, but it's close.

In seven years I've written nine books, accepted countless speaking engagements all over the world, run a household, and always had Christmas, Thanksgiving, and other various family dinners at my house. (That's what I get for having the only house big enough!) Christmas has always usurped tons of my time—partly because I have this thing about giving handmade gifts at Christmas, and partly because I go to ridiculous lengths to make Christmas very special.

This kind of scheduling has been going on for years, and it has taken an enormous effort to organize my time to be wife, mother, and writer. As a result, there is very little time to develop close friendships with a lot of people. And—make no mistake—friendship does take time and cultivation if it is to survive the productive, active years of our lives. In fact, you could name my closest friends on one hand and part of the other.

That's funny. I would have thought (because I feel like I know you) you would have literally thousands of friends all over the world.

Oh, in that sense of friendship, you're right. I do meet many people, and during some months of the year, I meet one or two thousand a week. But even if these people share that lovely common bond of Christ with me, the more appropriate word is not "friendship," but "acquaintanceship."

A friendship must be a give-and-take, two-way-street relationship. Acquaintanceship is generally just one way, or at best, limited in some manner. For instance, it's quite possible to live next to your neighbor for 10 years, but never invite him in for dinner with your family. That's acquaintanceship—*not* friendship. The difference lies in the fact that friendship requires—no, *demands* much more of a relationship. It's a little like the difference between dating and marriage. Dating goes along by itself, but marriage has to have commitment in order to survive.

Obviously you feel strongly about friends and friendships. Perhaps you could define some of the qualities that make friendship possible.

All right, but remember as you read my definitions that a friendship must be reciprocal. If only one person has these qualities, it is not a friendship. A relationship? Yes, but a friendship? No. It's more likely to be a student-to-teacher, client-to-counselor, employee-to-management or child-to-parent relationship and not a friendship in the fullest sense

1. I think a friend is a person whose face lights up with a sparkling glow when *you* walk into a room.

I can remember going to the airport several times to pick up my long-distance friend, Clare Bauer. (To my regret, she lives both out of town and out of state.) I have seen her walk down the steps of the plane, look about, see me, and break into a sunshine-filled, joyous look. I'm told my face mirrors the same look back to her. No matter how many times I see special friends, I notice that same look of joy, and I feel warm and blessed all over again by that friendship. When your husband is your *best* friend (as mine is to me), or your children have grown into your friends (as in my family), then this look happens each time you see each other, and it renews the ties of love.

Actually, animals are better at this nonverbal communication than humans. Our dog Sidney greets each member of the family with his own individual brand of gladness, even if we've been gone only five minutes to take the trash out. Sidney cannot contain his joy when my husband gets home in the evening. In fact until Dick stoops down, pets him, talks to him and ruffles his fur, Sidney will not stop his jumping, barking, and running. He is our friend and he's joyous to see and greet us.

2. I think friends continue, year after year, to be a never-ending fountain of encouragement—in spite of the fact that they know you. They always seem to be an oasis in the desert of your dry soul. They can be perfectly well aware of your weaknesses and your slightly undesirable character traits. But they like you anyway. Real friends (God bless them all!) do not dwell on your human shortcomings, but concentrate on accepting you as you are.

In 1 Thessalonians 5:11–12, we read that we should "encourage one another, and strengthen one another" (AAT) and appreciate (or honor) the workers among us. In short, this passage tells us how to make friends—and how to keep them.

For the past four years I've been involved in *Family Forum* seminars in many parts of the United States with Dr. James C. Dobson, psychologist and author. One of the delights of working with this gifted man is his practical, ever-expanding ability to encourage me to be the very best woman of God I can be. He does it by giving clear, honest evaluations of my work, by verbally patting me on the back, by accepting me as I am, and by willingly communicating to me a loving, Christlike understanding. Within this framework we are free to iron out conflicts when they arise, to be tired or discouraged when we feel that way, and in general to be used of God beyond our expectations.

3. I feel a friend should be one who prays for you, whether you need it and deserve it or not. And a friend should be your godly, spiritual "advice giver" as well.

I don't know if I agree with you on that last part

*about "advice giver." Over the years I've been so
hurt by some Christians that I don't think I'm
ready to cope with any more spiritual remarks.*

You're missing my point. I said a *friend*, not just
any acquaintance, should fulfill this function in
your life. When I'm searching out God's will on a
certain matter, I have several routes available to
me. First, I go directly to God in prayer. Then I
check His Word with my life to see if I am con-
sistently obeying Him and keeping His commandments. (That's how we really show our love to
Him.) Finally, I check with godly friends. The
psalmist tells us, "Blessed is the man that walketh
not in the counsel of the ungodly" (Ps. 1:1). We
are not to rely on our acquaintances or unsaved
friends in times of directional, emotional, physical,
or spiritual need, but on prayer-motivated friends.

When Marion Miller died, I lost not only my
mother, but my best—my very best—friend. Years
later as I was sorting out my loss, it occurred to me
that our strongest bonds were forged out of her
fantastic prayer life. This is still the quality of
friendship I miss in her loss and the same one I
look for in new friends. The absence of her prayers
has left my heart bare and lonely, but in time God
has seen to it that I have praying friends. They
have helped fill up the empty spaces in my heart,
and they have done it by prayer.

I have found, too, that you don't really need a
whole lot of close friends who pray, but like the
hair tonic, "a little dab will do ya." You do need a
few, though, who really connect.

4. Finally, I'm quite sure a friend is someone
who would not give up on you, even if you called
in the middle of the night to relate a shocking, ugly,

devastating detail about yourself. A friend would not abandon you for one single split second.

How many friends could you make such a call to?

Ah . . . maybe four.

Great! That's about two ahead of most of us. I don't know how it happened, or who started the rumor, but having *lots* of friends is just not where it's at. If you have two or three friends in your whole lifetime who can be counted on, depended on, and prayed with, you know what the real essence of friendship is all about. Quality counts in friendship far above quantity.

In the few really close friends you have, is there one quality common to all of them, or are they all very different?

Well, they are different in that I have a different relationship with each one. And since one of them is my husband and others are my children, there are bound to be differences. However, they all share one trait—a trait I identified just lately, and only by accident.

Recently I was asked to be the chapel speaker at Azusa Pacific College. My brother and sister-in-law, my sister and brother-in-law, and now my daughter-in-love, Teresa, have all graduated from this fine Christian college. I've been doing chapel services there for the last ten years, but this particular morning as I sat down before chapel, Teresa gave me a letter. (She's in her fifth year, finishing some student teaching courses.) Here is part of her letter:

Dearest Joyce,

I'm so proud of you! All week I've been so excited because MY mother-in-love was going to be in chapel. You're such a special speaker, not just because you are dear to me, but because of your message and the pain you go through so that others might truly have a clearer glimpse of Jesus. [I have a painful problem with my jaw involving the joints, teeth, and facial muscles.]

I'm really praying for your jaw, but sometimes it's hard to talk to God about it when I know He could stop the pain. Funny, how we are all learning how to trust the Lord with this. . . ."

Naturally anyone would love a letter like this one. Teresa began it by encouraging me (one of the essentials in being a friend—remember?). Then she conveyed the message that she's hurting with me over this jaw problem. I'm very pleased that she didn't give me some pat answer or a spiritual cliché about my pain, but frankly let me know it troubles her. (It troubles me, too.) Then, near the end of the letter, she wrote, "I guess the best way to tell you I love you is by telling you—*you are my best friend* (—next to Rick)."

I don't mind being second to her husband, especially since he's my son!

Several days after I read her letter, I was thinking about my very extra lovely friendship with this precious girl. Actually, I was driving to the grocery store when I wondered aloud why Teresa's friendship is so special. It occurred to me that one of her most outstanding personality traits is her eagerness. That girl is eager and ever so desirous of being God's person, 100% of the time, every waking hour of her life. It was while I was pushing my shopping cart down an aisle at the store that I realized, "not only has Teresa an eagerness about life, but so do my husband, daughter, and my closest friends. They all want, more than anything, to please God by being His obedient children. They continually rush into each new day to see just how God will work. They don't pretend to have all the answers, but their outlook is filled with *eagerness* to be what He wants them to be.

This is the main quality I look for in a friend, and while my friends have different temperaments and ages, with different backgrounds and cultures, their eagerness to be God's people is always visible and recognizable.

Colossians 2 deals with friendship and with Christ. Read it. It's really beautiful. Down about the sixth verse, Paul reminds the Christians at Colosse that they've trusted Christ with their salvation; now they are to trust Him with their daily problems. And he ends by telling them to "live in vital union" (LB) with the Lord. I've paraphrased "vital union" as "eagerness" in my Bible because eagerness is the essence of the vital union of friends. It is also a trait I see in all of my dearest friends.

3

Loneliness—
Living With It

I am a basically happy 23-year-old woman, and I'm at peace about taking a new job many miles from my family and hometown, but I do experience loneliness at times. I realize I am not unique with these alone feelings, yet that does not seem to eliminate the pain. Do you have any suggestions for coping with loneliness as a single adult?

My first reaction, off the top of my head, is to remember I'm happily married, have loving kids (who are my best friends), and am surrounded by dear ones. I wonder what possible suggestions I could give you from up here in my ivory tower, out of touch with the reality of single adulthood. But the next reaction, which takes longer, is to come to grips with the problems of thousands of young and old people alike who face being alone in this world.

The segment of our society known as "single

25

adults" is composed of people in every age bracket from youth to senior citizen. Here are three factors—to name just a few—that have caused this group to grow by leaps and bounds in the last decade:

1. The death of a loved one
2. A divorce
3. The ever-growing belief that marriage is obsolete

Death, of course, we have had for all time, and divorce is escalating. But the relatively new factor—the idea that marriage is quite unnecessary—has propelled an astounding number of young adults into single living.

We are going to have to give serious attention to the problems associated with single "bliss," and I see real progress beginning to be made. For instance, there was a time when not one book in a Christian bookstore dealt with singleness. But that situation has changed, and I predict we will see more books on this subject as time goes on. Some concerned churches are turning with gifted insight to the problems of the single adult, and it is a joy to see how God is blessing.

Many churches have single adult Sunday School classes now, and they are beginning to plan innovative activities which involve singles, old and young, in community and church-related projects. Also we are finally beginning to recognize the needs of the single parent. In our own church we have a gifted wife and mother teaching women who are single parents the how-tos of raising children. Still other churches and concerned Christians are just beginning to be aware of the vast, virtually untouched ministry to the widowed, divorced, and singles within their congregations.

As I see it, the need for ministering will only grow in the coming years.

Back to your question of coping with loneliness. Remember, we all suffer from loneliness, no matter who we are or what our status is. The trick is in recognizing it, coping with it, and accepting it as a part of life.

Paul believed we should be content in whatever state we find ourselves (Phil. 4:11), including the state of loneliness. This advice isn't patronizing or glib; Paul meant it and he spoke from painful experience. He had known the "state" of being shipwrecked, of being manacled in a dank, dark jail, of being sick, and of being lonely a long way from home. He did not ask us to do anything that he had not already tried and come through.

Paul took his example of "accepting our state" from our Lord.

To live out a situation and accept it—whether we like it, love it, enjoy it or hate every second of it—is to follow Jesus' example during his 40 days of testing in the wilderness (Matt. 4). I doubt that any human being in the history of mankind has ever been lonelier than Jesus.

To know that my gracious Lord knows firsthand the depths of my isolation, the feeling of loneliness, gives me courage to accept my state.

The problem of being young and single is that just about the time I begin to accept my singleness, some well-meaning lady says, "My, my, what's a nice girl like you doing not married?" She tends to make me lose my cool!

I can understand your frustration with ladies like that and with others who continually play the matchmaker role without your approval. But try to remember—most older people were raised with marriage as the only acceptable goal in life for a woman. Don't be too hard on them; it's their background.

I have the terrible urge to tell them to mind their own business, but I know that's really not too swift. Can you give me something a little more constructive to say?

Yes, not only to say, but to grasp as a concept. Listen to Paul's words: "I'm not saying you must marry; but you certainly *may* if you wish. I wish everyone could get along without marrying, just as I do. But we are not all the same. God gives some the gift of a husband or wife, and others he gives the gift of being able to stay happily unmarried" (1 Cor. 7:6–7, LB).

Some of the most talented, creative, and used-of-God people I know are single. Of course, they have their times of deep loneliness, but they have "the gift of being able to stay happily unmarried" and they are a delight to everyone's heart!

All right, besides accepting my singleness, what else can I do?

You've put your finger right on it, and it's a word only two letters long: DO.

When Margaret Landorf died, my father-in-law was devastated, cut in half, and couldn't think of many reasons to continue his life here. Since his wife had been such a close companion, her sudden death during an afternoon nap plunged him into a sea of loneliness that he'd never known before.

When I talked with him he told me of the pain of loneliness. Over and over again I suggested things for him to do. Things like traveling or taking up golf—but he didn't seem to be listening. Then, after about five or six months of his grief-stricken loneliness, I asked him again how he was doing. There was a long pause, and then he said, "Dear, I guess I'll just have to *do* something about my loneliness." It was his turning point.

Now, months later, nothing's really changed except his attitude, and he has been making great strides. I don't mean to imply that his loneliness has vanished—it hasn't—but he's working on getting out of himself and *doing* something about his state. God is gradually healing him.

Much emotional healing comes when we lose ourselves to reach out to others. It comes when we care about someone else's load, and when we show appreciation for someone else's talents. Giving ourselves to others is a healthy way to come alive again. My darling father-in-law is just now experiencing this new life. His cheeks are rosy with his joy and his eyes are beginning to dance with laughter again.

I hear you telling me to accept loneliness and to do something about it. Anything else?

Definitely. *Use it.* It may mean thanking God for loneliness when you've never done that before. Sometimes when we thank God for a problem, He shows us its real value. Your experience with loneliness may be the very tool God uses to bring real "beauty out of ashes." But the process begins with thanking Him.

When you mentioned the pain of loneliness, you

immediately took me back to an event in my child-hood. Let me give you some background.

Until I was 13, I was an only child, so my adoles-cence was, as I remember it, an *alone* time. Also, because Dad was a minister, we moved 5 times before I was 10. This meant we moved every two years, made new friends, lived with both grand-mothers at various times, and changed schools with nauseating regularity. It was not—and I really mean this—*not* a sad, lonely childhood or one I brood about in my memories, but it was one of aloneness. Some interesting and meaningful growth occurred without my notice at the time, but now, as an adult, I appreciate the lessons I learned. I am utterly grateful beyond belief to our Lord for those precarious, rather scary years. (Hindsight seems to be one of my better traits!)

After the outbreak of World War II, my mother and father took up jobs in factories while they worked to start a new church. The wages from those jobs gave us extra income we'd never had before. And so when I was 10 years old, we did the grandest thing we'd ever done: We built a modest little house and moved into the very first dwelling place we had lived in that was not a walk-up-three-flights rental flat, a dreary parsonage, or one small room at Grandma's house! It was a whole new house, all our own, and moving into it was a joyous experience! My father had an artist paint a sign that was hung in the house as soon as the rafters were built. It read:

"A carpenter can build a house,
But only God can make a home."

During the first year in our new dream home, with both my parents working, I got to know lone-liness firsthand.

The day you made me remember was a day like many before. I came home from school to the cool and empty house, changed my clothes, snacked on something, and began piano practicing. I had a million things I wanted to tell Mother about my day—not that they were as important as the European news of the war—but they were very important to me, and it was disappointing that I couldn't share them. By suppertime, when she would be home, I would have forgotten what had been burning on my tongue to tell!

I began my piano practice with an organized review of scales, but boredom took over, and I slid easily into a kind of practicing which can only be described as "messing off."

Someone outside started a game of kick-the-can in the street, and I could hear my friends choosing up sides. I knew I couldn't join them because I hadn't practiced enough. (Even if the word "practicing" was a poor choice, it had to be done.) Feeling extremely sorry for poor hemmed-in me, I sat on that piano bench cushion of self-pity and went back to my lesson. The game outside was over or had moved to a new spot by the time I finished, so I idly picked up one of our hymnals and began playing each song, as best I could. (Actually, I stuck to those written in the key of C. An absence of sharps or flats lowered the error factor a bit.)

There I was, 11 years old, surrounded by a nicely furnished home, the sounds of friends fairly close by, and the tried and tested songs of the faith coming out of my piano. But I was overwhelmed by how very alone I was; I wished for my mother or dad to walk in. I wished to see my cousins. I wished for someone—or a bunch of someones—to bring me out of this aloneness. But no one came.

Then the strangest thing happened. As I concentrated on the music in front of me and sang the words to a hymn I can't recall now, I was aware that I was not alone. God's presence filled every available space and, at first, it frightened me. Pretty soon I stopped playing, began to cry (my life motto: "When in doubt, cry"), and finally said out loud, "Lord, is that You?"

As I recall, He didn't answer me; but it didn't matter. I knew it was the Spirit of God, He was real, and He was there with me.

I certainly did not put this lesson into words that day, but years later the message of the afternoon seemed to be "I'll be lonely again, but I do not ever have to be *alone*. And there is a difference." That day, as I grew a little more accustomed to the Lord's presence, I finally found the courage to ask, "Was there anything You wanted to say to me?"

What was said in the next hour was deeply personal, yet not filled with details, dates, places, or plans; only a deeply moving conversation with God about my life's direction.

I was still at the piano long after 6 when my mother came home. She took one look at my tears and flew at me with, "Honey, Honey, what's the matter? What's happened? Why are you crying?"

I blurted out, "God was here all afternoon."

It didn't seem to startle her at all. She just asked, "What did He want?"

"Me, I think." And a lovely knowing smile gentled her face.

"Tell me everything," she said.

I really couldn't explain it all except to tell her someday, sometime, somewhere, somehow, and by some means, God would let me share in His ministry, His suffering, His work, and others would love and come to know Him because of me.

She listened, nodded, smiled, and said, "Oh, my" and "How wonderful of Him" a lot, and then tucked it all quietly inside her soul.

Later, at 15, I began a rebellion and a rejection of the Lord which did not end until I was 25 and nearly a suicide statistic. I'm quite sure Mother often reached into her soul's pocket and longingly looked at the promise of a visit from God.

I am honestly convinced that learning the lessons of loneliness and knowing aloneness so many years, and at such a young age, did more to prepare me for the traumas of adulthood than any other childhood experience. There is a peace that comes from understanding the difference between loneliness and being alone—a peace I feel when I lean back and allow God to spend the afternoon in my soul. It has come flooding back into my tired heart as recently as last week during a long flight home on a crowded jet airliner. And perhaps, just perhaps, I am the woman I am today because of yesteryears' times of loneliness. You know, if that's even half true (and I'm sure it is), I should be praising and thanking God for that lonely childhood, the constant moving, the never-ending making and breaking of friendships, and the long, quiet hours spent listening to Him.

I've never thought of thanking God for my single life-style, but maybe it's the very conditioning I need to help me really reach out in love to others who are hurting because of their loneliness.

You're absolutely right, and you've just stated some real ways to cope with loneliness:

1. To say with Paul, "I'll be content in whatever state I am."
2. I'll accept my situation.
3. I'll DO something outside myself about my loneliness.
4. I'll thank God for even this loneliness.
5. I'll use my loneliness as a tool to reach out to other lonely souls with Jesus' love.

Did many people in the Scriptures have problems with loneliness?

They certainly did. The Bible doesn't use our specific world "loneliness," but it's there in story after story. There isn't space or time here, but I've always thought I'd like to do a study on many of the Old and New Testament people in regard to their times of aloneness. David, in his childhood, for instance. What more lonely job than that of a shepherd? Yet those early days of his life were probably the very times when the psalms were forged. I could write of Moses, Abraham, John, and others and about the way God used their loneliness and how they used it to become the people God wanted them to be. When you think that God did that for them so long ago, isn't it great He still does it today!

Your daughter Laurie is almost 21. Is there some book (besides yours, ha!) which she has found particularly meaningful as a single girl?

Yes, again and again she has come to me and said, "Mom, just listen to this . . ." and then she has read from a devotional book called *Come Away, My Beloved* by Frances J. Roberts (The King's

Press, 1970). She said yesterday, "That's a book you can read and reread all the time." If you get a copy, you'll see how very personal it is, as though it were written just for you. Two pages entitled, "I Anticipate Thy Dependence On Me" are before me now, and I have the very personal feeling that they were written for me today.

I pray God teaches you the art of coping with and using loneliness in a creative way, and that you will understand, fully, that you are not alone —*ever!*

4

Suffering—
Part of Our Calling

I'm a little depressed at all the suffering I see going on around me. What bugs me the most is seeing good people suffer. I don't handle that too well.

Neither did the Old Testament Prophet, Habakkuk. He puts it well: "O Lord, how long must I call for help before You will listen?" (Hab. 1:2, LB) Then he talks to the Lord about unfair law and judgment practices and pours out his heart about suffering of all kinds.

I think none of us handles the problems of suffering too well, especially if it's hitting very close to home, or if it's happening to a Christian friend.

To me, it seems so unfair of God, especially when you see giants of the faith suffer and die with cancer while the crooked businessman or the affluent prostitute appears to be in the pink of health.

36

Actually, it has nothing to do with justice or how fair God is. Rather, it has everything to do with sin and man's rebellion against God. The God I serve does not sit up in heaven gleefully rubbing His hands together while He plots whom He's going to punish or kill off next.

God does *allow* suffering (rather than *send* it) and many times He does *not* tell us the whys or the purposes. Usually the not-knowing really gets to us. We want answers to all our questions, especially when we are experiencing losses of any kind.

I take it, then, you don't buy the old song which talks about God's answering all our questions once we get to heaven.

No, I don't. I can't imagine taking all the incongruities of my life (our son's death, the pain in my jaw, the loss of a great mother) and putting them in a little brown bag to take to heaven. Nor can I see myself in the midst of heaven's glories, climbing up into God's lap, opening my little brown bag of whys and saying, "All right, now, why did You allow this?" Our Lord promised us that He will wipe away all tears in heaven, and I think He must have a way of wiping our questions and hurts from our memories as well.

Besides, when you read the complete book of Job you'll notice that at no time does God *ever* explain the whys of Job's terrible, hideous sufferings and losses. Not even after Job has been restored to health and position does God shed any light on the purpose of Job's tragedy. But God did allow it.

Since you have had suffering in your life, do you have any pet peeves on the subject?

I'm afraid I do. There are many causes of suffering—divorce, physical pain, death of a loved one, for example. And there are different responses to suffering—mental anguish, grief, frustration, hopelessness, and bitterness, to name just a few. So it's impossible to have one easy answer that fits every occaion. That's why some of the things which are said by well-meaning Christians irritate me so much.

Like what?

Like a trite little quote, a Bible verse taken out of context, or a sermonette, given by a Christian who at that moment is *not* suffering and, in some cases, *never* has.

Do many people do that?

Yes, an appalling number of people feel "led" to share their thoughts, with devastating results. I think I've been guilty of doing the same thing myself, though, and I can easily see how it happens.

When we are *not* in the actual process of suffering, we feel no pain. Our spirit is not crushed and defeated, our faith is riding high, and our presence of mind is relatively good. So in our blissful condition we issue little "good news" bulletins to others with nauseating regularity. It's a whole different ball game when *we* are in the process of suffering.

The pain, whether it's mental or physical, blots out our abiilty to reason. It cripples our spirit with discouragement (particularly if the pain has gone on a long time) and we lose our balance in regard to a perspective of life. Spiritually, some days, we take breathtaking trips into high realms of God's glory, and then plummet deep into the darkest part of depression without a moment's notice. Such is the nature of pain.

If the pain of suffering does all that to a person, isn't that the very time we need to remind him of Romans 8:28? ". . . all things work together for good to them that love God, to them who are the called according to His purpose."

Not necessarily. What we need to realize about the mystery of suffering is that when we are in the midst of acute suffering our minds and hearts are simply incapable of taking Romans 8:28 at face value. We are at the same place, physically and spiritually, as Jesus was in Gethsemane when he pleaded, "Father, if Thou be willing, remove this cup from Me; nevertheless not My will, but Thine, be done" (Luke 22:42). The verse which follows tells that an angel ministered to Him. Yet, He was still suffering because the very next verse says, "And being in agony He prayed more earnestly; and His sweat was as it were great drops of blood falling down to the ground" (v. 44).

To have reminded Him that "all things work together for good" would have been highly unnecessary. He knew the final outcome. He knew the bottom line. But He still suffered and "his cup" was *not* removed.

For other people to pat us on the back with Romans 8:28, especially when they are not in pain, is the height of hypocrisy and phony love. It is hard for me to say this because I know someone is bound to say, "Joyce is against using Scripture." But that's not true. I just know from experience that it is one thing to have a nonsuffering Christian quote Scripture to me, and it is entirely different to wake up in the middle of the night in acute, pounding pain, and to hear the soft voice of our Lord whisper, "My Child, this will all work out for good because you love Me and are called for My purposes." There's quite a difference! One is an outer command and does nothing but make the sufferer feel guilty because he or she didn't quote it first; the other is the kind of inner urging from the Lord that heals.

What should our position be then, as Christians, in regard to suffering?

First of all, we need to take a better look at suffering, and I don't mean *only* the physical kind, but the mental and emotional as well. Often a large part of our prayer list is made up of requests to get us out of our suffering, as if it's a plague to be avoided at all times.

Peter tells us, however, that suffering is a part of our work or calling (1 Peter 2:21). In fact, God places great value on suffering. The Scriptures tell us that suffering is a necessary ingredient in our spiritual development.

When I looked up the word "suffering" in the concordance, I was astounded to see column after column of references under "suffer," "sufferest," "suffereth," and "suffering." I looked up many of the verses, and I was quite surprised by the Bible's emphasis on suffering as the key to obedience, growth, patience, and even fellowship in our lives.

Somewhere along the line we have preached or implied that God does not want us to suffer, ever; not physically, not mentally, and not emotionally. That simply is not true, especially in the light of the Scriptures which tell us what God can and does do through our heartaches and agony.

I hear you saying that perhaps I should stop asking for the Lord to remove all suffering, and accept it instead, on the basis that it may well be an important part of my growth and development as a Christian.

Exactly. This position may get me into trouble with my Christian brothers and sisters who insist God wants everyone well. However, I know God does not want a little girl named Kelly to die of cancer, but He may allow her to die of cancer to carry out His will for her and glorify His purposes.

To be alive is to experience suffering and death. It is not what we *might* suffer; it's a fact. We *will* suffer, and how we handle suffering and how we allow God to use it in our lives is what makes the difference.

Are you saying we should not pray for healing during our suffering?

No, of course not, because God *does* heal. But I want us to get back to the biblical principles of suffering and to accept the possibility that at this time God *may not heal us.*

Do you really believe God uses ugly, horrendous suffering to glorious ends?

I have to believe that with all my heart, especially since I've talked to hundreds of hurting people and I have experienced my own pain. I *have* to know (deep down) there is a godly purpose in the seemingly tragic injustices of life, or I would lose my mind.

God says that I am to glory—not endure—but glory in suffering and tribulation, and concentrating on that command keeps my sanity. I know nothing of really being a disciple of Christ, but suffering is like taking a full semester of classes, a summer school, and a correspondence course on discipleship—all at the same time.

You said in Mourning Song, *your book on death and dying, that we need to use grief as a creative gift. Do you believe that about suffering too?*

Yes, but when I'm in the middle of real intense suffering I tend to believe it a little less! However, the *truth* of it always remains.

The great, real poems of Annie Johnson Flint and Martha Snell Nicholson are just two examples of work which was sculptured out of the rock of suffering.

My pastor, Dr. Ted Cole, reminded me of a well-known truth on suffering when he said,

"There is no oil without squeezing the olives,
No wine without pressing the grapes,
No fragrance without crushing the flowers, and
No real joy without sorrow."

The Dale Galloway story is an excellent example of suffering that produces a creative gift. You can read the details in his book, *Dream a New Dream* (Tyndale House Publishers, 1975), but here are a few high points.

Dale was a young minister of a growing church when out-of-the-blue his wife divorced him and took their two children with her. In the months which followed, all his efforts to save the marriage failed, his church eventually turned him out, and he thought he would die from his lonely broken-ness.

God reached through the pieces of this man's soul and tenderly made Dale a brand new, whole man. God restored Dale's purpose for living, but I doubt his book could have been so powerfully writ-ten without the intense suffering he endured to produce it. I deplore the heartbreak of divorce and all Dale went through. I wish he could have been spared it, yet I see what God did overall and I cannot contain my joy!

What can we do for someone who is suffering, without being trite or sermonizing?

As my friend Keith Korstjens says, we can "loan our faith" to each other.

When I am in maximum pain, my faith is not merely at a low ebb; it has, in fact, ebbed com-pletely away. I don't seem to be able to stockpile a large deposit of faith, and pain is one of the things that quickly eats away what little faith I do have. It's interesting that I can find faith for some-one else's needs if the occasion calls for it, and I have no problem believing God *will* intervene. But my own pain makes my faith vanish into thin air.

The faith and prayers which friends loan me during the severe part of my suffering have brought me through more than once. Just today my father telephoned. His prayer and his complete faith in Jesus' ability to touch and heal me came at the right moment.

How I love the story of the man suffering from palsy who was brought to Jesus by his friends. Remember? They couldn't get him inside the house

where Jesus was teaching so they did the un-
thinkable thing. They tore up the roof tiles and
let him down through the hole. They had pooled
and loaned all of their collective faith to the sick
man and when Jesus saw *their* faith (not the man's)
He met the need (Luke 5:18–20).

I am frustrated by glib comments about God
when I am suffering, but when a friend loans me
his or her faith and in great love prays for me, ah,
then I am restored.

Praying and loaning our faith to others are not
the only things we can do for suffering. We can
help them accept their illness, pain, loss, or whatever by empathizing with them.

Empathy is described in the dictionary as intel-
lectual or emotional identification with another
person. My husband identifies *with* me when he
takes my face in his hands and says, "Oh, Hon, I
wish I could have this pain for you." Both he and
our children have prayed for me, and my pain has
done something for their spiritual growth, but it is
their empathy with me that reduces panic during
extreme pain.

My friend Linda, who knows more about pain
than I do because of the fused and deteriorating
disks which have produced arthritis in her back,
told me of the effect empathy had in her life one
night.

She and her husband had been watching television, but she had been unable to get into a com-
fortable position. She had been on the chair, the
floor, and the couch, but was driven to complete
frustration by the pain.

Finally, reduced to tears, she said, "Ray, what
am I going to do about this pain? I just can't
stand it any longer."

Her husband reached over and instantly turned off the television set. Looking directly at her, he said, "Linda, the only thing I know at this point is that we are doing everything that can possibly be done and from here on, you'll just have to 'gut it out.' When it gets so bad you can't handle that alone, remember—*I'm right here.*"

Linda is not out of pain, she has not been healed, and her situation has not changed, but she is accepting her suffering (no easy task). Her husband's words of empathy are part of God's restoration in her life.

Is there a verse (OK, I know it's not Romans 8:28) that is especially meaningful to you when you are suffering?

Whoops, I see I'd better correct something here. I didn't mean to come down so hard on Romans 8:28. It *is* one of my mainstays during pain. However, for *someone else* to steamroll this verse over my head when I'm so sick I cannot see, much less think, is very cruel of him—or her.

The promise that "all things work together"— even when all things seem to be splitting apart— has been beautifully confirmed deep in my heart by God Himself, as I have already said.

My friend Brenda said, "That's it! *Confirmed* by God. Other people don't need to sermonize to confirm what God has already shown you!"

Here are some verses which are taking a high position on my priority list for suffering.

"For I know the plans I have for you, says the Lord. They are plans for good and not for evil, to give you a future and a hope. In those days when you pray, I will listen. You will find Me when you seek Me, if you look for Me in earnest" (Jer. 29:11–13, LB).

Another verse which has helped tremendously: "I know you well, you aren't strong, but you have tried to obey and have not denied My name. Therefore I have opened a door to you that no one can shut" (Rev. 3:8, LB).

5

Divorce—
A Closed Door

In your book For These Fragile Times *you wrote an article about two women who had both lost their husbands of over 20 years, one by death and one by divorce. I read the article in somewhat of a detached frame of mind, but found it interesting, anyway.*

Since then, however, out of the blue, my husband has left me and within a few months our divorce will be final. I never dreamed this would happen to me. I feel abandoned and betrayed. How am I to be both mother and father to our two children, and will I ever get over the confused frightened fear which grips me the first thing every morning?

It would take too long (and too many pages) for me to tell you how deeply touched I am by your hurting heart. I don't know if I can help, but I'll try. I think we are talking about doors which have closed, and the problems of adjusting to them, and looking at the new room in front of us.

Are you simplifying my divorce by merely call-ing it a "closed door"?

Forgive me if I seemed to minimize the enor-mous problems of divorce, but I do believe that a "closed door" is *anything representing a normal way of life or living which is abruptly altered or cut off from us.* When something once wide open to us is slammed in our faces, I don't think it's an oversimplification to call it a closed door.

When I think of our marriage, I could just cry.

Go ahead. Closed doors are always hard to un-derstand. Crying is one of the best tension relievers around, and certainly to cry is *not* a sign of spiri-tual weakness.

Yes, crying maybe, but when I panic that's a sign of spiritual weakness, isn't it?

Absolutely not. Christians who say there has never been a single moment of panic in their lives are either lying or living in a cover-up fantasy world. We all panic. However, as practicing, obey-ing children of God, we usually panic on the "biggie" issues, and the duration of that panic is considerably shorter for us than for non-Christians. In the middle of my panics, I repeat, "This, too, shall pass," and it reduces the panic level some-what.

I wish I could understand the whys of closed doors like this divorce. Would it help if I knew and understood how, when, and why this all happened?"

I doubt it.

Just today I read an article about a woman who had lost the use of her right arm in a freak accident. She wrote a graphic, descriptive account of how limited her world had become, but she concluded by wanting to know *why* it had happened to her.

Long after I finished reading, I kept wondering two things: (1) Would it have helped, really helped, her to accept it had she known why? (2) Would it have changed anything or given her a new arm? I had to say "no" to both points.

I honestly don't think knowing the whys and the hows of things helps or changes a situation. Yet we persist in the middle of the emotional upheaval of "why." Continuing to ask the question is nothing short of emotional suicide.

All right, so I'll try to stop asking why and I'll re-read your chapter on suffering, but what can I do with this closed door?

You just used the magic word. Do. As I have written (and spoken) before, when we decide to *do* something, we are heading toward emotional health.

If you can, and I know it will be difficult, try to think, pray, talk, read, move, and function while you seek out closed-door possibilities.

That's easy for you to say because, even though you came to the point of suicide, the Lord restored your marriage, and you and your husband both

became Christians. I'm in the middle of a divorce.
You sound as if all I'm to do is to "think positively"
about my situation.

No. That would be very cold of me, and not
what I mean at all. Maybe this will help: (1) Only
the Lord knows why our marriage survived and
yours went down the tubes. He not only makes
each snowflake different; He makes humans different and individualistic as well. (2) I am not patting you on the back and glibly telling you to
think good thoughts about your devastating
divorce. No way! There's a lot more to my suggestion than that.

I think when a door closes behind us (whether
it's gently shut or slammed), we have to turn to
the *new room* before us and seek the mind of God,
beginning with, "OK, Lord, now—about this room
—what did You have in mind?"

After a door closed, a friend said to me, "I honestly believe God is telling me something, directing
me into some other phase of my life, and I love
Him for caring and leading so faithfully."

Stop and think right now about the possibility
that this divorce might be God's leading into a
new phase with Him. Don't be afraid to search
for His direction with all your heart. He can be
found.

Yes, but your friend was talking about a change
of direction. I'm talking about a mind-blowing di-
vorce, and there's quite a difference between the
two.

Is there? I wonder. When we are born-again
children of God, isn't *everything* that happens to us

under His control? His perfect will for you would have been a beautiful marriage, but evidently His permissive will has allowed a divorce, despite all your corrective measures. My friend, it's true, wasn't talking about *your divorce* when she said God was directing her into some other phase of life, but she was talking about *your same God.* Luke tells us that everything with man is impossible in life, but that *with God,* nothing is impossible (Luke 18:27).

I guess it's just easier to trust the Lord's everyday direction when we can see the road clearly ahead. But when it's dark and we are dealing with the emotional pain of divorce, we bog down. Other than zeroing in on what God wants to do in my life right now, do you have any more suggestions?

Yes. I pray God raises up some godly, unbiased-about-divorce friends—Christian friends who know the exact meaning of how God transmits His love through one human being to another.

In the beginning of this chapter, you referred to an article I'd written on two women. The one was widowed, the other divorced. Do you remember my prayer at the end?

Some of it, but not the complete thing.

Well, this is my prayer as I wrote it then, and it's still my prayer for now:

O Lord,
Two women have lost their husbands.
I do not understand the "whys" of either loss.
I find I am gentle, sympathetic, understanding,
And willing to bake cookies for one.

But for the other . . .
What can I say? What do I do?
She is half a person too, Lord.
Only it's hard to explain her loss to other couples,
    relatives, especially the children.

O Lord,
Both of these women are widows.
Give me a gentle compassion for them.
Not sticky sweet pity, but an open mind and a
    listening heart.
Help me not to prejudge the situation
    or hold myself up as a paragon of spiritual
    righteousness.
Breathe the right words for both women into my
    uncomprehending heart;
For I don't know any brilliant answers.
Their needs, Lord, stun my ability to comprehend.

So I bring both women to You and thank You
    in advance
For the healing which they both so desperately
    need.

After that article and prayer was published, first
in the *Power for Living* Sunday School paper, and
later in *For These Fragile Times,* I received many,
many letters about it. I asked one writer if I could
share her remarks with you and she wrote back,
"You may certainly use my letter in your book.
I've done just enough writing to know that when
God gives thoughts so quickly I can hardly write
them down, He has a definite purpose for those
words!"

Here is her entire letter:

Dear Joyce,

After reading your article, "Six Months Later"

in *Power*, I just felt I would like to share with you some of the most helpful things Christian friends did for me during my divorce.

I wish I could express how *very much* a divorced Christian woman needs love and the assurance that she is still accepted as a worthwhile person!

In every way possible, I had tried so desperately to save our marriage of 19 years. (My crushed, unworthy feeling was compounded by my strong convictions about the wrongness of divorce.)

One day, I walked into my pastor's office and asked, "What do you do when you feel like garbage?" He looked so kindly at me and said, "Remember God loves you *just as much* as He ever did." The reminder that God's love is not lessened by any wrong I had done, nor increased by any good works was my mainstay through the ugly months following the breakup of my marriage.

Incidentally, God always expressed that love through His people—a warm squeeze and a whispered, "I'm praying for you," as I would be leaving the sanctuary; the bag of perfectly lovely outgrown clothes for my children; the delicious roast from another's freezer; or the understanding person who invited my girls to stay overnight so I could "pull myself together."

I firmly believe that God has given His church a wide-open field of true ministry to divorced people if we will accept it. Over and over He has put suffering people in my path. They are not afraid to be real with me, because they know I can understand exactly the hurts, fears, and uncertainties they are feeling; I am privileged to share the all-sufficiency of the Lord Jesus Christ.

As for myself, in no other way could God so dramatically have shown me how everything *comes* from Him, everything belongs to Him, and everything is *safe* and all right in His hands.

After three and one-half years, I am just now beginning to thank Him for it all—for the sake of what this terrible experience has done to let me see and know Him and His ways in a way I have desired all my life.

Thanks so much for your books and articles! (I didn't expect to be so lengthy when I started; but please don't be afraid to reach out to divorced persons. They need the same Lord that married ones enjoy. And He is sufficient!)

Sincerely,

--- ---

As I read her letter, I heard her say four very important things, and I wish I could say them to each and every divorced Christian alive. I know it would promote emotional healing.

1. The person who is experiencing a divorce has a tremendous need to be assured of our love. The amount of loneliness, guilt, frustrating feelings of worthlessness, and lack of any self-esteem must be massive and immeasurable.

You see, here you are about to be a divorcée, with all the stigmas of failure surrounding you, all the past sins and faults looming up behind you, and all the question marks of the future before you. Naturally, you feel worthless!

While I have not experienced divorce, I do remember one quiet, desperate afternoon (*after* I was a Christian) when I felt something akin to these feelings of worthlessness, and it was then I found Ephesians 1:4: "He hath chosen us in Him before the foundation of the world, that we should be holy and without blame before Him in love." It has been my life verse ever since. I sign it beneath my name while autographing books and records, and it has rescued me from the pit of low self-esteem.

2. I loved the divorced woman's remark, "Incidentally, God always expressed that love through His people." *We need each other.* As I've already said, I pray God raises up some *real* Christian friends for you.

3. Who knows. Maybe, like other divorcées, you, too, will have a ministry among others who hurt as you have hurt. Don't be surprised when God puts broken, fragmented people in your path and then gives you the loving wisdom to heal them.

One of my most cherished letters is a scribbled note on the back of a program from a woman who had experienced one of the worst "closed-door" situations anyone could have endured. Her lovely 17-year-old daughter and boyfriend were both murdered. Her note describes a little of her year-and-a-half of anguish at their death, and the horror of the murder trial as well. Then she wrote these revealing words, "Your book *Mourning Song* is the first help for my bitterness that I have found. What you have said today has opened my heart for the first time. Perhaps with your help I will be able to start trying to heal the wounds of my husband and three children."

I could never have written a book on death and dying without losing my son David, my grandfather, and my precious 57-year-old mother. Their deaths have given me a ministry to heal the emotions of the grieving as nothing else could have done.

Your divorce may give you an awareness, an empathy, and an understanding such as you have never known before, for others.

4. Finally, did you notice it was three and one-half years after the letter writer's divorce before she could praise God, thank Him, and gain any insight into His ways? This kind of maturing in Christ and this kind of emotional healing does not come overnight. God heals, but often His healing is gradual rather than spontaneous. Don't be too hard on yourself, or too impatient with your slow recovery. Just remember, He *is* healing. The scar tissue may hurt for a long time, but He is healing just the same.

Thank you, Joyce, I'm beginning to lose some of my panic and, if you'll excuse me, I think I'll take another look at the possibilities of my "closed door."

6

Singleness—
It Scares Me to Death!

I am in college, I date some guys, but I've never found a "Mister Right." Frankly, the thought of being single all my life scares me to death! I am possessed by the fear of living life as a single person. I am afraid that I'll grab the first male that comes along because I feel so desperate about remaining single. What can I possibly do to overcome this constant, dreadful fear?

If you continue to let this fear dominate all your thoughts, it will destroy the one thing you don't want to lose—your attractiveness to available men. Fear cripples us. It will fade that lovely face of yours into a twisted, anxious mass of worry lines. Who likes to be with a fearful, tense person (male *or* female) for very long? Not me, and not you. Yet your fear can cut away your vocal chords so you can't speak. It can dry up that dewy sparkle in your eyes, which makes you so attractive. In the end, it can make you a drab, dull young woman who will be highly undesirable.

You said, "If you let this fear dominate . . ." I'm not letting it; it simply is.

Yes, I understand how fear does that, but when we allow fears to take over our thoughts *always,* we stand dangerously close to having our fears become phobias. I wish you'd read chapter two of my book *The Fragrance of Beauty,* the chapter on fear. I think it would help.

What's the difference between a fear and a phobia?

Well, let me share one of my fears with you, as an illustration. I am afraid of snakes and lizards. I always have been, and I don't mean a mere dislike of them, but a definite, paralyzing fear. It doesn't matter that the garter snakes or lizards we have in California are far more afraid of me than I am of them. They still scare me silly! However, I'll know my fear has gone from fear to phobia if I become so preoccupied by the fear that I stay inside, or will not look at a picture of a reptile, or will not visit a country, a home, or a zoo which might have snakes. My fear has become a phobia if my mind is totally taken up with avoiding snakes.

Then, how do you handle this fear of snakes?

First by admitting that I *do* have a problem with the fear of snakes. Somehow it took me years to admit it and not feel terribly guilty about it.

There always seems to be some loving soul who blesses me with the information that most snakes and lizards are harmless, which only adds to my guilt.

Second, I will not allow this fear to become a phobia. In no way do I want a phobia to rule and dictate the way I live my life, and phobias do exactly that if you let them.

Third—and this may sound corny, but it's true, nevertheless—I've had to turn my fear of snakes over to the Lord, which wasn't easy because even the thought of a slithering snake sends a chill through my brain. But I must live, I must go places, I must be about my purpose for living, and I have to face the fact that I just may run into a snake or two along the way. God is going to have to give me the courage of the moment when it happens.

Just before I spoke and sang for the Army in Panama a few years ago, someone (bless him!) told me of the large iguana lizards of Panama. I remember Don and Perky Brandt coming over to our house to say good-bye to me before the trip. We were all teasing and talking about my trip, especially since there had been a rash of airplane hijackings, when I said, "The only thing that really scares me about flying to Panama is the snakes and iguanas." We were all so noisy I didn't think anyone heard me. But all of a sudden everyone was quiet because Don was saying, "I think we ought to pray about that." His prayer was simple, direct, and sensible. He told the Lord about my fears, asked Him not to let me see one single snake or iguana, and finished by saying simply, "Lord, if she sees one snake, it will keep her awake all night, and she needs her rest to do Your ministry there."

The Lord really answered Don's prayer because I was in Panama seven days and never once saw a snake, lizard, or even a worm. The very last day, however, Alice Meek, the chaplain's wife, took me to the plaza to shop. We walked by some low bushes and Alice kept bending over looking under the bushes muttering, "I can't understand this at all!" Finally I said, "For Pete's sake, Alice, what are you doing looking under those bushes?" Her answer gave me the double reaction of instant heart failure and complete resuscitation! She said, "Well, I didn't want you to leave Panama without seeing our famous iguanas, and this is where just tons of them live. They are harmless, you know, but today I can't find a single one!"

Ah, yes! I knew exactly why they hadn't come out. *They wouldn't dare!*

OK, so I admit my fear, watch that it doesn't become a phobia, and turn it over to the Lord. Sounds simple enough. But tell me, how can I really "turn it over to the Lord"?

By being willing to be *you.*

But I am willing to be me!

No way, Lady. You're willing to be *you* up to a point, but you're not willing to be *you* if it means being single. You're saying, "God, I'll trust you with my schooling, my job, my family relationships, but not with my future regarding a mate. This I'm gonna worry and fret about."

I have a long list of things I'd like to be or have either now or in the future. Things like having the vocal control of Barbra Streisand, the long career of Kate Smith, the glow of Dale Evans, the spiritual insights of the late Henrietta Mears (and my mother), the figure of my daughter Laurie, the blue eyes of my daughter-in-love Teresa, and Dinah Shore's afternoon TV show, but I am *me* not them. I'm faced every morning with being Joyce Landorf. I have her gifts, her problems, her strengths, her weaknesses, her loves, her fears, her husband, and her family. I can either accept her as she is or continually pine for all those other attributes God has given someone else. I must be willing to be me *all the way.*

The sooner you accept your singleness, the quicker you relax and become involved in being God's person; then, look out because when you least expect it, Mr. Right *may* pop into your life.

Does sitting down on your fear and doing what you're supposed to do actually relieve the terrible fears and tensions of being single?

I could tell you a lot of stories about how this works. One concerns a girl named Andrea and a boy named Tim.

Andrea's sister, Judy, was suddenly taken seriously ill and for some time she hung between life and death. God worked in Judy's surgery and is even now gently restoring her life. The whole Lakatos family was involved in Judy's recovery program. Her hospitalization was in Houston, Texas, and as Judy progressed, her sister, Andrea, left the family home in Michigan to be with her.

Andrea was not thinking in the least about getting a husband, and certainly had no idea she would meet him in Houston. But here is what happened, as Andrea's mother wrote me:

Would you believe that Judy's illness was the method God used to bring Tim into Andrea's life? Tim was visiting *his* sister in Houston and saw Andrea wheeling Judy down the hall. (He had quietly been calling himself Hansel and had been looking for his Gretel.) When he saw Andrea, he whispered to the Lord, "*That's* my Gretel!" He hurried over to Andrea, introduced himself, and quickly added, "I'm a Baptist—what are you?" They couldn't believe they were both (first) Christians and then Baptists! As Andrea told me later, "When you do the trusting, God does the working."

What's so special about Andrea and Tim is they were both doing what they were supposed to be doing. They were not desperately searching for a mate; they were not fearful about the future. They were simply in the right place at the right time, doing exactly the right thing. God saw their trust and obedience in Him and wrought a miracle in a hospital corridor for both of them.

I'm getting the message, Joyce. Once, when I heard you talk, you mentioned in passing that your daughter has a list of 20 things she'd like in a husband. Could you list 20 points as guidelines for me?

I'll be glad to give you her general areas as a guide to follow. But you should draw up your own list to fit yourself, your circumstances, and your God-given calling.

The first five qualifications are the top priority on her list; hence, they are the beginning five. They have everything to do with:

1. *Spiritual Qualifications* These specify that a

mate be a Christian, and outline his attitudes on the importance of praying together, on Bible study, on church attendance, on spiritual instruction for children, and even on tithing and serving the Lord and His church.

The next five qualifications involve:

2. *Background and Family Experiences* The family upbringing, whether wholesome or fragmented, is very important to the health of a marriage. Some backgrounds, because they *were* horrendous, make great adults. But other people never overcome a broken home, alcoholic parents, or being an orphan. Also, it's important to ask how you and your fiancé fit into each others family life-style. You don't marry just a person; you usually marry all the relatives as well. Every Christmas, Thanksgiving, or birthday event can be pure heaven or excruciating murder. So you should examine cultural beliefs, eating habits, social manners, and certainly, future goals for your own lives and the lives of your children, should you have any.

The next five qualifications are about:

3. *Educational and Future Employment Standards* A girl with a college degree can make a marriage work with a guy who dropped out of school at the eighth grade, but it will be a constant struggle.

A young man who is brilliant in physics and sciences of all kinds married a young woman who never finished high school. Two years and one child later, when they divorced, he complained, "She reads only comic books!" He said he never figured that the lack of schooling would be so important, and he was shocked that her reading level was so low.

This set of five questions should also include the type of employment you both will agree on. Are you willing to be the wife of a lawyer, doctor, minister, or someone in another pressure-cooker calling? Or are you willing to be a farmer's wife in rural America—or perhaps a miner's wife up in the wilds of Alaska? What will you be able to add to his work as the helpmate God wants you to be? These and other questions should be thoroughly talked over, including the attitudes both of you have on working wives and mothers.

The last five qualifications deal with:

4. *Physical Appearance* As you can see, this category is at the bottom of the list. Laurie wants a husband with blue eyes. I did too, and my mother before me! However, if a brown-eyed man comes along who has all the other qualifications, these are the five points she'll eagerly compromise. The top five—the spiritual qualifications—are the no-nos, the not-to-be-tampered-with part of her list. At times this policy has cost her some pretty good men. However, she has seen firsthand here at home how important those top five are, and—bless her —she's holding out until she finds all those spiritual qualities in a man.

I wish you were my mother. I know you're not, but if you were, what single piece of advice would you consider most important to give me?

Never settle for second best. Be willing to be you, to obey God, and to wait for God's first choice! Is it worth it to wait for God's first choice, even if you have to wait a long time? In the words of my friend Carolyn Balch, who married at 30, "you betcha!"

OK, but let's consider that marriage might not be for me.

Then I would still give the same advice. I know many single women who will probably never marry, yet who *have* "God's first choice" in their lives. They live productive, amazing lives, and I sincerely feel if they were married they could not do all they do or give their jobs the immense attention needed for the tremendous results they get.

So . . .

Be willing to be you,
Obey God, and
Wait for God's first choice.

7

Dinner Hour—
Disaster or Delight

It was easy to see, as I read Mix Butter With Love, *that you felt very strongly about two things: mothers-in-law and dinnertime. I have a great mother-in-love so I don't need help in this area, but I am interested in improving our dinner hour. Could you explain with a little more detail why you feel the dinner hour is so critical in meeting the needs of a family?*

I guess it's so special because it's the hub of the family wheel. It's the very center, the one time when the family puts down its various schedules and comes together. Sometimes it's the only time we see all members of the family together at one time.

But what of those years when you have infant babies, tiny children, or absentee teenagers, and coming together for one meal just isn't possible?

There is a fact that never changes, and that is the fact that the family is always changing. We start out single, then pair off, grow, expand, decrease, and over the years very little remains the same. However, all through the changing years, there are those times, those years, and sometimes only those moments when we can make dinner very special if we want to.

Let's talk about the babies and small children problems first. Obviously, you can't have a lovely, organized, fun, yet calm dinnertime around the table as you could if your children were older, so accept the limitations of their ages. Babies are known for their talent of crying between 5 and 7 P.M. Little children's low blood sugar bottoms out during these same hours (sometimes earlier), so until they are older, the main motto for dinner has to read, "Be flexible!"

Yes, as I recall, my two children drove me right up the wall around 4:30 every afternoon, and since we didn't have dinner until 6 or so, I was a sunset wreck. How could I have avoided some of those drastic days?

By recognizing the children's grumpiness and bickering as a time to change something—*anything!* You could have given them a glass of orange juice, cut up an apple or orange for them, or even given them a quick bath right then instead of later before bed.

My mother used to give my children those little individual boxes of raisins at the first sign that everybody was falling apart. In earlier days, before the boxes, she gave me handfuls of raisins. I don't think she ever knew too much about fatigue and low blood sugar. She just knew raisins worked.

While your children are under five years of age, you may want to feed them early. You will feel as if you're making two sets of dinners, but the alternative of waiting for Daddy and dinner with quarreling, cranky children may outweigh the work. When you and your husband eat later, you can let them have dessert or snacks if they show a desire to eat with you.

At the other end of the spectrum of raising a family, you may have teenagers who are so active and involved outside the home you might not know they live with you if it weren't for all those dirty socks and jeans. They hold down jobs, go to school, and are active in church and sports. If you have more than one teenager, you're back to making two dinners or more per day.

I recall that during our family's growing time, I made dinner for our son Rick at 4:30 P.M. because he had to go to work. I made dinner for Laurie at 5 o'clock because she was off to a church function. I ate at 5:30 because I had a speaking engagement somewhere, and I left a full dinner for my husband Dick because he would not be home until after 7 o'clock. It was a time for flexibility, and obviously we did not have a glorious sit-down dinner, except occasionally on Sundays. However, we knew it couldn't last forever, so during that year—while Rick got awfully tired of frozen chicken pies—we cheered each other along, and we all survived.

Is the job of making the dinnertime special solely up to me as the wife and mother?

Not completely, but it's conceivable that it may have to start with you. And, of course, unless you're wealthy enough to employ a cook, your meals and table settings will be up to your creative imagination and abilities.

How does my husband fit into making our dinnertime a time to remember?

He has a lot to do with it. But you must talk with him about your desire to make the absolute most out of this brief time. Explain your feelings about wanting a good mealtime memory for all of you, and enlist his support.

Where do I start with my own attitudes about dinnertime?

Begin by remembering your own childhood and the dinnertimes in your memory. Ask yourself questions like these:

1. Was dinner a time of happiness?
2. Was the food fixed attractively and nutritiously, whether there was a scant amount, or plenty of it?
3. What were conversations like? Were they mind-stretching, informative, and fun, or were they critical, filled with yelling threats or active with disciplining?
4. Did you go to the table dreading the confrontation, or hungrily anticipating the food and people?
5. What was the rule for table etiquette? Were manners and kindness practiced, preached, or nonexistent?
6. Was there a centerpiece, a flower, or a candle to dress up the table?

Answering questions like these will help you to

see how *you* are building memories for your children. It will point out the glaring mistakes or the beautiful successes which have been made, and you can learn from those memories. What will your children recall about your dinnertimes some 20 years from now? It's good to go back in time and see the good and the bad of your childhood, and then use the lessons you learn!

If it's not too personal, what are your childhood memories of dinner and food?

I have several distinct sets of memories. Because we lived with my grandmothers for a short time, many of my memories are of delicious meals at their houses.

My Hungarian grandma always had something cooking on the back of her stove—maybe chicken soup or stuffed cabbage—and her house always had a marvelous smell because of that back burner. In fact, "simmering" was the first cooking term I ever really understood. Grandma's house smelled like love, and it's a rich memory for me.

My Irish grandma, on my dad's side, gave me special memories too. She would make a pot of tea, pour out a cup, add a bit of milk and sugar, and then she'd put me on her lap. I'd get to sip tea from her cup. Even though I was very young (and everyone said coffee and tea would stunt a little child's growth), I can still remember being snugly held, listening to her loving chatter in my ear, and having our very own little tea party together.

My memories of the dinner hour are mostly from the age of seven on. Dinner was never very big in quantity, but because of my mother's creative ability it ranked 100% in quality. She cooked balanced meals of meat—tuna was a favorite—potatoes or rice, and vegetables, and always served a salad in her original style. Money was scarce so necessity became the mother of many a creative invention in our kitchen.

My memories of conversations through the years are not the best.

My parents were dedicated to the Lord in a superspecial way, and we all ate, slept, and breathed Christianity. My dad was called to the ministry when he was very young, and to this day he still is a fine pastor. Each dinner, lunch, or breakfast, the conversation was always about Christians, Christianity, or some other church-related subject.

It seemed to me the conversations were more negative than positive. The church people and their problems, the church building with its shortcomings, the church board with their difficulties were usual dinner fare. I'm sure now it was never done on purpose; it just seemed to be a habit we fell into early in our lives. Also, our church-centered conversation was enhanced by a phone call or two during dinner from members of our congregation each night. I cannot remember ever talking about my world, my mother's world, or the world in general. The topic of conversation always had to do with the church world.

Did that make you feel angry toward the church or your dad's work as a minister?

No, not right then, but it certainly did when I grew into my teens. By then I think I really believed all Christians were neurotic—always in hot water or in some kind of crisis situation. Our dinner conversations thoroughly convinced me of that.

How do you feel about those conversations now?

When I was 25 years old and had become a wife, a mother, and a Christian, I reexamined that background very carefully. Fortunately, the Lord healed the hurts of those memories, and instead of being bitter or upset about those depressing conversations, I made up my mind very definitely on one score: Our present and future dinner hours would have widely variegated subjects and would not be like those of my past.

You know, it's funny, but our past experiences can keep us all bound up, repeating the same failures over and over again, or they can motivate us in the opposite direction. We have the ability to let the past serve as a lesson, rather than a pattern, for our future.

It's highly possible my cookbook and this chapter would not be nearly as meaningful without the particular dinner conversations we had back when.

Our time together in this life is so brief that I don't want to miss anything going on in our family. I don't want a dinner hour spent in useless critical conversation, or in bickering, disciplining, or sarcasm, because it's really only a snap of the fingers between diapers, bridal gowns, and cemeteries.

My children are 6, 8, and 11 years old. So I guess they are old enough to retain memories of our dinnertime. But I'm still not convinced that

*mealtime is so terribly important to the develop-
ment of the family, other than nutritionally.*

Many, many marriage counselors, psychologists,
and psychiatrists would disagree with you. But
what really convinced me *I* should do something
about our dinnertime was the fact that Jesus made
a big deal out of eating together.

He performed His first miracle at a wedding
feast (John 2). (They didn't have cake, punch,
mints, and nuts at the reception. They served many
courses of food and it *was* a feast.) Eating with
the families of the bride and groom was an important part of the ceremony.

When Jesus called Zaccheus down from the
tree, He didn't take him to the temple; He invited
Himself over for dinner! (Luke 19)

Then there was Jesus' concern about feeding the
five thousand (Luke 9:10–17). He knew the people needed to eat. He understood the necessity
of food for their bodies, their minds, and their
emotional dispositions.

I find, too, that when Jesus wanted to give the
message of holy Communion before His death, He
chose a dinner to reveal this sacrament (Matt. 26).
This meal is called the "Last Supper," implying
that Jesus and the disciples broke bread together
many times during His three-year ministry.

Even after He arose from the grave, He ate with
the two men on the Emmaus Road (Luke 24:13–
35). And He Himself cooked the fish on the beach,
showing His disciples He was flesh as well as spirit
after His resurrection (John 21).

I think, though, my favorite verse for really
doing something about dinner is Revelation 3:20:
"See, I'm standing at the door and knocking. If

you will listen to My voice and open the door, I will come in to you and eat with you, and you with Me" (AAT). Of all the things He *could* do, our Lord chooses to eat, to dine, to have dinner with the person who lets Him inside. The thought of our Lord eating at our house boggles my mind with wonder. At the same time, it makes me seriously question if our Lord would like to eat at my house in view of our food, our manners (or lack of them), or our conversations.

I think I've gotten the message: dinner is important. Now, pretend I know nothing of how to go about making dinner special. And be practical, please.

First of all, I'd have to say, "Learn to cook."

But I'm so bad at cooking that it seems the more I do it, the worse I get.

Since I got a D in home economics both semesters I took it, I can certainly share your anxiety. But, believe me, if you *want* to cook you'll be able to find the right book for recipes, or the right people to watch as *they* cook.

When I was teaching creative cooking to some Azusa Pacific College students, I found I was not able to teach them cooking until I taught them attitude. Once they wanted to try and were willing to make mistakes, they all became above average cooks!

Find a cookbook you can read and understand. If the terms and utensils are completely foreign to you, you've probably picked up a French gourmet's guide to gastronomic delights, and you need to settle for a lesser book written in English. You'll find simple-to-make but delicious foods in *Betty Crocker, Better Homes and Gardens, I Hate to Cook Book,* the compiled recipes of your church or club, and even my book, *Mix Butter with Love.* Start with one of these books and follow directions carefully, using the exact ingredients. You can improvise and substitute things later in your cooking career, but for now, do it as the book says.

Incidentally, your children are at the right ages for you to teach them to cook. Both boys and girls should be given a working knowledge of the mysteries of the kitchen.

I tried that once, just to get out of a little cooking activity, but the mess they made was more than the help they provided.

What happened to you was a very normal experience with mothers. Most of us teach our children to cook, but neglect to *teach* them the *other* side of cooking, which is cleaning up. Also, we start with dishes which are too difficult. Teach your six-year-old how to make really good toast. After he's mastered sliding the butter gently across the top of the toast without reducing the bread to one-sixteenth of an inch in thickness, show him how to mix cinnamon and sugar for a delicious topping. Then be sure you teach him to clean up the crumbs with a sponge or wet paper towel, since that's a part of making good toast, too.

While I'm still on learning to cook, let me make another suggestion. If your budget is *very* low, it will pay you in the long run to invest in a cookbook which deals with budget meals, or one which has 195 ways to make hamburger and beans. It seems to me we had years of no meat other than ham-burger (or tuna), and those books saved my sanity. Besides, they introduced our family to eating many *different* varieties of food.

Okay, I'll rearrange my attitude toward cooking and learn to cook. So what's next?

Serving and setting. I used to slop the food down any old way on the plate. I'm sure it hinders digestion as well as a happy feeling because it doesn't look too swift. I know it's going to get all messed up together once it gets inside, but when you put food on the plate, do it as artistically as you can. You can even color-coordinate foods by placing orange carrots next to white fish, or use green beans beside meat balls and spaghetti.

Then there's the setting of a pleasant table. I've written a whole chapter in *Mix Butter with Love* on "Flowers and Candlelight" because they are so vital to the dinner hour. They add and enhance our time together even if it's one flower and one candle. Placemats and napkins (paper will do nicely) and a table which is dressed up for the occasion says, "It's good to be here with you all!"

If, for any reason, you are eating alone, or if a child is sick, still set a pleasant table or tray. Today Laurie is in bed recovering from the flu. I made up her breakfast tray with a placemat, a small dish of scrambled eggs, a glass of orange juice, silverware, a napkin, and a glass vase with two daffodils and some baby's breath I stole from my kitchen table. The effort to make a pleasant tray was incredibly worth it all when she looked up at me with red, blurry eyes, and said, "Oh, Mom, how pretty!"

All right, now, after cooking, setting the table, and serving, what do I do about atmosphere and conversations?

Here we have the *heart* of dinner, so let me give you three things to mull over.

1. By *example*, teach manners. In private, and before dinner, you and your husband should agree on some basic manners you want to teach your children. Elementary ones such as chewing with the mouth closed, passing salt and pepper, and establishing the seating arrangement. You may also want to consider whether or not Dad should pull out Mother's chair, or if one of the older boys should do it. How will the meal be served, and how will you handle seconds? All of these considerations, and many more, are just exercises in *kindness*. That's really what manners are all about. The small courtesies are the most neglected acts in most families today.

The New Testament has a lot to say about etiquette and manners, but we don't notice because the Bible calls them "kindness" and "love." More Christian families than I care to remember are extremely unkind to each other at dinner, both by manners and by conversations.

"Please," "thank you," and "I'm sorry" are still magic words, and we need to teach them to our children and review them in *our hearts* as well if we are to practice New Testament Christianity.

2. Set the no-knock policy for dinner. Make it off limits to chop each other, to discipline about a past negligent act of the day, or to criticize one member of the family or some outsider. So many things are better left unsaid—at least during dinner!

Proverbs 15:17 says, "A dish of vegetables where

there's love is better than fattened beef with hate" (AAT). *The Living Bible* puts it another way: "It is better to eat soup with someone you love than a steak with someone you hate." And the King James Version talks of a "dinner of herbs where love is." The message is clear: We must put down our passion for chopping and knocking each other, and actively practice having a time to love during dinner.

We must not jab the needle of criticism or discipline into someone's most bruised and sensitive spot, because doing so completely deflates his feelings of self-worth. Your children will fuss and fume at each other to varying degrees, but you can at least hold a moratorium on such behavior at dinnertime. I am not saying we should never discipline our children or say anything negative, for there is a time for correcting and training. But there should be one sanctuary in the day in which we directly control the fervor or fairness of what we say to each other.

By the way, the no-knock policy goes for you, the parents, as well. If I burn a casserole (and I do about once every three months), I do not stammer out my apology and compound my failure. I simply say, "Tonight we are having Black Bottom Casserole. You will eat only the top half because the bottom half will poison you to death."

Back a bit you said we should "control" our words. Some things just slip out and I can't seem to control them, much less keep them back.

Yes you can, if you want to badly enough. In her book, *What Is a Family?* (Revell, 1975), Edith Schaeffer talks about this very thing—controlling what is said. She relates that after she fell and cracked or bruised her ribs, she learned very quickly to *control* her coughing, sneezing, and even laughing. I identify with her illustration because I'm just over a fall which gave me badly bruised ribs. I remember how many times I controlled all those breathing facilities; and I remember, too, how many times I said to my family, "Don't make me laugh. It just kills me!" You *can control* anything if you care enough or are motivated enough. It may be a daily decision, but you *can* decide to control the harmful words which so easily destroy each of us.

3. Lastly, structure what you and the family will say.

That sounds rather severe and rigid to me.

Maybe so, but hear me out. If you plan a series of relevant questions for your husband and children, you'll gain two advantages. You'll learn a lot about your family, and you'll have less time for criticisms and disciplining. The Bible certainly supports the idea that you structure conversations. Read Deuteronomy 6:4–9 and catch the importance of teaching God's commandments to our children at all times of the day. What better way to teach and to get to know them than by dinnertime conversation?

What kinds of questions should I ask?

Oh, questions like, "What was the happiest thing that happened at school (or work, or play) today?"/"What was the most unfair incident today?"/"Did you see God today?" (For a while our children didn't quite know how to respond to this one, until one day Laurie answered back, "Oh, yes. I saw Him in some pink flowers on the trees this morning." She'd just seen her first blossoming cherry tree.) Other questions like, "Did anyone say anything special to you today?" or, "What would you call today—a boring day, a good day, a fantastic day—and why?"

Proverbs 16:23 says that our conversation should be wise and should add to our learning. The next verse adds, "Pleasant words are as a honeycomb, sweet to the soul, and health to the bones."

You can be wise in forming your own structured questions, and if you do it all in loving kindness, you'll not only learn, but you'll bring "health to the bones" of your family.

It has been our family's experience that, though I started structured conversations, my husband, children, and relatives picked up the idea, and they have carried on the tradition ever since.

After her marriage to Paul, my sister Marilyn served her very first Thanksgiving dinner and invited both their families. She worked like a madwoman to make it just fabulous. Her table setting and food were just great, but the meal was almost a disaster. Just as the entire family sat waiting for grace to be said, the dog jumped up on Marilyn's lap and promptly threw up on her and also spoiled the table. By the time Marilyn had changed her dress, Paul had cleaned up the dog, and the table had been redone, everyone's enthusiasm for dinner was definitely dampened. Marilyn said she racked her brain for a few minutes to see what she could do, when suddenly she remembered "structured conversations at Joyce's house." She cheerily announced, "Now, we are going to go around the table while we eat and each one will share exactly what he is thankful for this Thanksgiving day." It vorked like a charm, and dinner was a smashing success. She recalled that it was just beautiful as they all began sharing from their different ages, perspectives, and experiences. In fact, it made the day. She turned the disaster into a time of "health to the bones," and the Lord has been blessing her table ever since.

Excuse me for rushing off, but I've got to go home and cook dinner, serve it, and enjoy my family for a change!

Go!

8

Trying to
Catch Christmas

Would you believe I'm not sure I want to catch Christmas?

Tell me why.

Well, I guess it's just that when I was a little girl, I could hardly wait for Christmas to come. In fact, I could hardly eat because of all the excitement during December. My memories of those Christmases are supergood, but everything has subtly changed over the years. Now that I'm an adult, I seem to have a deep resentment toward Christmas and I find my resentment growing each year.

I used to start dreading Christmas right after Thanksgiving. But last year I developed a distinct bad taste in my mouth just days after Holloween. I have the growing suspicion that my aversion to Christmas is going to begin somewhere between

*Father's Day in June, and the Fourth of July this
year.*

*Am I the only one who gets uptight and unrea-
sonably apprehensive over Christmas?*

No, hardly, but you are fairly rare in that you
actually admit it.

Disliking Christmas is sort of a secret disease,
and in a society where Christmas is *supposed* to be
one of *the* most fabulous times of the year, most
of us are not as open about suffering from the "Bah
Humbug" disease as you.

*I guess we really have no choice about Christ-
mas, especially if we are Christians. We are supposed to love every busy-busy, rush-rush minute
of it. Right?*

You're being too hard on yourself, but you are
right in many ways about not having a choice
about Christmas.

We are not helped by the media, in every form,
which present the message: "Christmas is the most
wonderful, happy, peaceful time of the year." In
reality, it's only a sophisticated campaign to get you
to buy everything in sight for the event. The TV
commercials at Christmas which get me the most
are the ones aimed at children which say, "Tell
your mommy this doll is *only* $19.98 at your near-
est toy store."

Actually, as Christians, our Christmas may be
celebrated as spiritually or carnally as we decide.
However, most of us cannot escape the peer pressure, the commercial messages, and the stress of
making Christmas something glorious, and we get
bogged down by trying to catch Christmas. We run

ourselves ragged trying to get everything done in order to make it a super wonderful time.

In the end, we find some people have a lovely Christmas, but we wives and mothers go through it in a daze.

Is that why Christmas has deteriorated into just one big month of endless headaches for me?

It may be. We have forgotten the enormous physical and mental toll we pay through hard work, decisions, and financial stress. Any one of these demands is headache material, but when we compare the carefree Christmas of a child with the responsibility-laden Christmas of an adult, the comparison is depressing.

Try to remember that most of the pre-Christmas cleaning, mailing, baking, shopping, wrapping, decorating, sending of cards, and paying of bills were done by your parents and, in particular, your mother. As a child you probably helped here and there, but the majority of the workload was on dear old Mom, and the bills were paid by good old Dad. Now that you are no longer free to sit back and enjoy Christmas like a child, the responsibility and workload can be quite frightening. I call this the "Christmas Cinderella Syndrome."

What's that?

Most of us wives and mothers behave like Cinderella: cooking, cleaning, and doing all the household chores, while everybody else dresses up and goes to the ball. Unfortunately, there is no fairy godmother to rescue us and no crown prince to take us away on his white horse. So some of us live out each Christmas with only a faint hope for better times in future years.

So my reactions, anxieties, and fears about Christmas are normal?

Very much so. We get so busy catching Christmas that Christmas never has a chance to catch us. I saw a timely cartoon the first week of December last year. A little girl had just spilled her milk and her mother had thoroughly bawled her out. The cartoon showed an older boy patting the girl's shoulder, saying, "Mom's not really mad at you, Ruthie. It's just the first sign that Christmas is coming."

We are all uptight about Christmas long before it happens, and unless we recognize this fact and determine to change some things, our dread of it will severely limit our ability to celebrate Christmas as our Lord wants.

Actually, when you come right down to it, even the practice of exchanging gifts is a large, horrendous, scary, and expensive task.

That's right. Haven't you decided on a gift for old Uncle Fudd, gone to the store, found nothing in his size or your price range, gone home, made him something, spent time, energy, and material, only to have him unwrap it on Christmas day and say, "My, that's nice. It's just like the one you bought me last year." Or worse, even before he puts it on, you know it's three sizes too small! I have *lived* the Uncle Fudd story and I've decided that wanting to turn in my "Merry Christmas" badge was one of my more rational feelings at the time.

I'm getting the idea you hate Christmas a little more than I do.

You could have said that about me a few years ago, but actually I do *love* Christmas now, and *all* its hassles.

What did you do to make that possible?

Well, a while back, I took a good look at what Christmas *was doing to me.* I was going all out for baking, making gifts, and doing all the things to make Christmas special, until I realized I was in a mental and physical stupor on December 24 and 25. I let Christmas fatigue me to the point of utter exhaustion. I am sure I was violating God's plan for my life every December. It was simply absurd to go so overboard and miss the most lovely celebration we have as Christians.

How did you change, then, so that you now love Christmas?

By practicing four big "don'ts."
1. *Don't miss Christmas.* I know this sounds like a contradiction, but hear me out. There are some years in our lives when we miss Christmas, and it's not our fault. For instance, I missed several Christmases because of illness or deaths in the family. Our baby son died right after Christmas one year, and I was in so much pain with illness before his death, I missed Christmas completely. Two Christmases later, my mother and grandfather were both dead, and Christmas was lost to me again. We can miss Christmas for a number of legitimate reasons, but my plea here is that we not miss an

ordinary Christmas by drowning ourselves in tons of preparation to the point of useless exhaustion and overdrawn bank accounts.

We can even go the other way on the spectrum and miss Christmas because of indifference and apathy. We can be so worn down by Christmases past and old activities that we go the opposite way and do *nothing* for the celebration of Jesus' birth. Christmas can be as elaborate or as simple as we want, but we should take a good look at what our celebration does to us in the process and then, by all means, try not to miss it.

2. *Don't Do It All Yourself—Share the Workload.* Your children can be drawn into a circle of love while you bake those special Christmas calorie goodies. If they are old enough, they can make their own cookies. And if the cookies are a success, they could be wrapped and given to Grandma as a Christmas gift.

Your older children can be elected to do special washing jobs like floors or windows. The mark of a good executive is the ability to delegate responsibility, and I think a mother must be just that kind of an efficient executive, especially in the Christmas season.

A wife's workload at Christmas is vast. Most of us get to the point of having made so many decisions, we can't decide whether to have hamburgers or tuna fish by December 15, so we need help.

Enlist your husband's help on buying gifts. It's a great idea to let him see, firsthand, the ways of a department store in the Christmas rush season. He could be responsible for shopping and buying a son's tricycle, a daughter's tennis racket, or a tool kit for his uncle.

What if your husband has terrible taste, or for some reason refuses to shop?

Then think of some other need you have that he can take care of, like getting the Christmas tree, putting up the outside decorations, doing the dishes, or shopping for groceries during those hectic weeks. You need to share the load somehow.

In the days gone by when people decorated the tree with strings of popcorn and cranberries, who do you think did all that work? Mother Dear? No way. It was a family project, and while good old Mother might have popped the corn and got things going, it was a joint effort for everyone. The workload was shared and, incidentally, many a happy memory was stashed away in the process.

This is just great. Is there anyone else I should enlist to share the workload during Christmas?

As a matter of fact, there is. Especially if Christmas dinner is at your house.

One of my most cherished childhood memories of Christmas is the dinners we had at my grandmother's house in Battle Creek, Michigan.

I remember sitting with my dad's huge family at one long stretched-from-the-dining-room-to-the-living-room table. I always searched out Aunt Hortense's potatoes, Aunt Ellen's red marshmallow and fruit Jello, my mother's Waldorf salad, and Grandma's golden baked turkey—*wherever* they were—and kept my eye on them so I wouldn't miss them. What a hubbub in that house as all those fabulous cooks brought in their treasures and laid them down in front of us. My father used to say, "Look at that table. It's just groaning with food!" Later, we'd eat so much we'd be the ones groaning! Everyone pitched in, cooked something, served something, and cleaned up! The spirit in which we did it was a joyous, loving one, and the memory warms my heart even now.

You know who in your family makes the best salads, who is a whiz at making delicious vegetables, who is a lousy cook and should bring the olives or rolls, and who makes pumpkin pies that melt away in your mouth. So ask them to do their own things.

There is no rhyme or reason to your having a large dinner for the family without help in either the food or cleaning up areas—unless, of course, you enjoy cruel and unusual punishment.

3. *Don't Miss the Fun and Joy of Christmas.*

Oh, dear. Now you've really put your finger on a sore spot. The fun and joy are very definitely missing in our house at Christmas.

They are missing because all of us get terribly caught up in the mechanics of getting ready for Christmas. There is so much for adults to do that we have little time left to play games or have plain old fun.

Finding time for joy at Christmas is a little like trying to find the time for a prayer life. If we wait until we *do* have time, we will never pray. We have to *take* the time and simply pray then. So it is with Christmas, too—finding or taking time to play is up to us. We need to take the time to enjoy Christmas.

Ask the Lord to help you be creative enough to make even simple baking tasks a fun thing.

I have often asked my audiences if they are fun to live with, and the reaction is always mixed. But when I ask, "Would you like to be married to you?" the answer is clearly, "No, thank you."

You may have to ask the Lord to extend your sense of humor to its outer limits, but do it. Christmas is worth it.

Take a good look at Christmastime in your home, survey the humor situation, and then relax! Even if all the work is not completed, all the cookies not baked, all the gifts not wrapped or delivered, the sky will definitely not fall down. Really.

One of the fun things we have done at our house for several years during the first week of December, is to clear off the coffee table and dump a huge picture puzzle down on it.

It's funny, but I've never *ever* asked anyone to please work on the puzzle, yet it is nearly always completed by Christmas. Having the puzzle out all month has a surprising, even soothing effect on my busy kids, husband, family, and guests. They all seem to gravitate to the coffee table in the family room. And no matter how much time they spend on the puzzle, they come away having enjoyed a quiet moment of fun in spite of the Christmas rush.

You mention "joy" as well as "fun." Give me a suggestion for putting joy into Christmas.

Simply never have a Christmas dinner without inviting someone who is lonely, bereaved, or without a family of his own, to eat with you and spend the day. Many families, my own included, have found this tradition brings a tremendous measure of Christmas joy.

This lovely Christ-centered tradition was given as a gift to me when I was 15, and I'll never forget it.

My father's mother died just before Christmas, so my parents had to go back East for the funeral. We had just moved out to California and didn't know too many people, but it was arranged that I'd finish the last few days of school and then spend the holidays with Nancy Roy, a girlfriend from church.

Tearfully, my parents left our apartment and drove back to Michigan for Grandma Miller's funeral.

I had gone to Nancy's church, but I knew very little of her parents. As it turned out, her whole family were marvelous people. Nancy's father, Dr. Roy, was then president of Westmont College, and Mrs. Roy welcomed me as if I were just another well-loved daughter.

When I questioned Nancy about my wonderful treatment, their love, even the little gifts I'd been given, she just shrugged it off by saying, "Oh, Mom and Dad always have someone in over Christmas. Mom doesn't think *anyone* should be alone. Besides, she says *we* get the biggest blessing when we share our Christmas." I'm convinced, now, that Mrs. Roy knew the joy given would never exceed the joy received. Her Christmas tradition was based on the promise of Luke 6:38: "Give, and it shall be given unto you; good measure, pressed down, and shaken together, and running over, shall men give into your bosom. For with the same measure that ye mete withal it shall be measured to you again."

It's been almost 30 years since the Roys befriended a very lonely 15-year-old girl, but the joyous impact of that Christmas still burns brightly inside of me.

From then on, my parents had someone in for Christmas and other holidays as well. And, when

I was able to have Christmas dinners in my own home, I continued the tradition, and it has always produced pure joy!

Now, tell me the last "don't."

4. *Don't Expect the Impossible.*

Many times we set up in our memories a "perfect" Christmas and from then on we compare each Christmas to that one. It's absolutely insane, but we do it just about every year.

Did you have a perfect Christmas memory to compare Christmases with?

Ah, yes! When I was 10, I wanted, more than anything else in the world, a pair of white shoe skates so I could go ice skating. My dreams all came true on Christmas when the house smelled of goodness, love, and fir branches, and my grandparents gave me the *exact* special skates I'd longed for, pined for, and dreamed of. Christmas was perfect, perfect, perfect!

It's foolish, I know, but for years I wanted every Christmas to be like that one. Yet everything changes, time marches on, and it was highly frustrating to find none of my Christmases matching up to that one back in 1942. I was guilty of expecting the impossible and was constantly being hurt or disappointed.

What other things would you call "expecting the impossible"?

Oh, things like expecting changes from an alcoholic aunt who always spoils every family occasion by being drunk and obnoxious. Or a brother or sister who whines in self-pity during each Christmas dinner. Or, worse, one who is critical of everything you do or serve. Or, maybe you have a mother-in-law who checks your closets to see how good a housekeeper you have become in the years of marriage to her son.

All the above family-type problems are figments of my imagination. But all of us have people in our lives who will never change, yet we continually expect them to, and of course that's expecting the impossible!

The most important rule of good, sound mental health is to change the things you can change, but accept the things (or people) you cannot change.

After I spoke to the women of the Cradle Rockers group at our church last December, one of the young mothers said, "I really needed to hear your point about 'don't expect the impossible.' I have an alcoholic sister who has upset me and every family occasion for years.

"You're right, too, about my spending my lifetime expecting her to change mysteriously and be sober for once. She's never sober and I'm always disappointed, hurt, and left with a whole lot of bitterness inside my soul.

"I can hardly wait until Christmas. When she comes in, stoned and glassy-eyed, I'll remember she has never been otherwise, so I'll accept her as she is.

"The only thing wrong with your talk, Joyce, is that I should have heard it before Thanksgiving this year."

Accepting her sister will not be an easy task for this woman. Faced with a real-life situation like this one, we should apply Ephesians 4:32: "And be ye kind one to another, tenderhearted, forgiving one another, even as God for Christ's sake hath forgiven you." Here in this verse we find the power to forgive and accept others as *we* have been forgiven and accepted.

I guess every family gathering has rugged individualists, mean or critical, unregenerate or deeply sinful, mentally or physically ill, and even crying babies or spoiled children. So what counts is how readily we accept them.

That's very true. We have a friend who expresses his own unhappiness by acting highly critical of us when he is in our house.

Some time ago we realized that he's frustrated about his own life (not ours) to the point of wanting no one else to be happy, to have material things, or to cook better than he does. So when we invite him for dinner, we *expect* him to be critical.

It's become fairly exciting because we wait all during dinner for him to find something wrong and, sure enough, he rarely disappoints us.

When he is critical of the soup, salad, or whatever, I say, "You know, you are probably right." It's a good line to remember. The Scripture, "A soft answer turneth away wrath" (Prov. 15:1), is not only good for the hearer, but the speaker as well!

After our friend has been critical and I've said my now-famous line, I can catch any number of winks and smiles from our family. We all know he's said what we expected, and he probably feels better. To expect a different type of behavior would be a continual source of hurt. To expect his criticisms as his problem, not ours, frees us to love and accept him—*as is.*

Yes, that's like buying a dress on sale when the price tag is marked, "as is." You look the dress over and find a split seam, two missing buttons, or a broken zipper, and you buy or don't buy the dress—depending on whether or not you'll accept it as is.

You're right. It's also true that when our Lord saved us He did it while we were in the "as-is" state. He *never* gave us a six-month probationary contract to see if we'd shape up and change our life-styles. He forgave us when we came to Him, *as is*, on the spot. We must remember this when we are trying to forgive and accept a member of our family or some friend who leaves a lot to be desired.

A letter in front of me is from another young mother from our church. Part of it reads,

> Dear Joyce,
>
> As I was praying for you today, God reminded me I had not told you how much I appreciated your words at the Christmas meeting of Cradle Rockers.
>
> You really zeroed in on my need when you spoke of not expecting the impossible.
>
> Every year as Christmas approaches, I have a dream of entertaining so elegantly! I see the entire group being so grateful, warm, and harmonious. Then comes the disappointment of reality.
>
> Well, this year you helped me face Christmas *realistically* and while it was one of the most difficult, it was one of the nicest ever!

Her letter sums it up very well.

Before I quit on this subject of Christmas, I must

include a very appropriate poem. It has been written by a delightful 73-year-old grandmother named Doris L. Van Meter.

Catching Up

I can't catch up with Christmas
No matter how I try.
I stand at the cross street
And watch the crowd go by.
Inside, the press and hurry
And rush leave me amazed.
I almost fear to enter,
My senses are all dazed
I think I'll find a house of God
And stay on bended knee,
Till I have calmness in my soul
And Christmas catches me.

(used by permission)

The lady who wrote that poem is very wise! I'm beginning to see Christmas in a different way. I'm going to let the Lord catch me with His kind of Christmas.

I think I'll find a house of God
And stay on bended knee,
Till I have calmness in my soul
And Christmas catches me.

9

Unlimited Corners

Recently I heard you speak at a women's retreat. For me the day went all too fast. I especially wished you would have gone into more detail about your sister Marilyn and her complicated first pregnancy.

Since I am five months along with my first baby, you can understand my interest.

Many things you said about Marilyn, her husband, Paul, their life together, and now this pregnancy, were very similar to our situation, so I really identified with her.

Could you elaborate a little more on a term you used when you summed up their problems? You called it "the unlimited corner." What is that?

Actually, it's the name of a darling gift store owned by Jane Mackinnon's niece in Coolidge, Texas.

I was in the process of unwrapping a gift from her store when I saw the wording on their lovely gold label, "The Unlimited Corner." I thought,

"Isn't that exactly where God puts us a lot of times!"

From that day on, I've thought of Marilyn and Paul's situation as the unlimited corner of God's direction. They may not be in their favorite place—it's just a *corner*—but their hope is in the word *unlimited* because that word describes God's ability to forgive, His power to bless and direct, and His freely given grace to keep on keeping on.

You said they are living in Kentucky now.

Yes, after they both graduated from Azusa Pacific College in California, they decided to further Paul's education as a minister. Right now they are at Asbury Theological Seminary in Kentucky, and Paul is a few months from graduating.

I don't imagine they are too financially secure.

You're quite right.

In a time when the cost of living is so high, how do they handle economic pressure while they go to school?

Two ways. One, by going without a lot of things *I* think are absolute essentials (especially nonfood items like nail polish and camera film); and, two, by keeping a detailed, precise, absolutely-kept-to budget.

They knew that it would be almost impossible to take a three-year seminary course in two years with very little visible means of support. But both of them felt the Lord wanted Paul to further his education before entering the ministry full time.

Here, I think, is one important key to living in God's will daily. They united in prayer, examined all the alternatives, talked with Christian leaders, searched their own souls and motives, reviewed the impossible corners the two years would hold, and then did what they felt was God's bidding.

In other words, they went into those precarious two years of financial insecurity with their eyes wide open.

Exactly. They did not have two different sets of opinions, goals, and priorities. Instead, they were unified as they approached the problems together. They were well aware that they had a rough road to travel, but they stuck to their plan, and they stuck together.

My husband and I have made plans that we thought were God's will, but the whole situation has turned out to be one big failure. How could this have happened? We both felt our decision was God's will.

I don't know all the details of your failure, of course, but sometimes we tend to make decisions based on our feelings alone. Perhaps when I said Marilyn and Paul did what they "felt was God's leading," you may have assumed that they were motivated by just their feelings. In reality, there were many other factors. As I said before, their *feelings* about God's direction were preceded by lots of homework, soul-searching, talking, testing, and united praying. The "feeling" part came after a good many months of fact-finding. It came like the caboose on a train—at the end. The engine in

front was teamwork, and it preceded the caboose
by many a car length of work.

Their church sends Marilyn and Paul a helpful
monthly check, and on occasion their income has
been supplemented by friends and relatives. Paul
has secured loans but, all in all, it has been nip and
tuck financially for them during these two years
of schooling. However, never before have I seen
two people enjoy such rapid spiritual growth. God
is definitely using all this experience in their lives.

It's been interesting to watch God come through
at every crisis point. Each time they've been in an
unlimited corner experience, God has intervened,
and they have recognized His miraculous ways in
no uncertain terms.

Give me a "for instance" or two.

All right. Let's start with finances. The first year
of Paul's tuition was taken care of by a gift from
his grandmother. But for this last year he has
worked part-time and has taken out loan grants.
Also, Marilyn worked in the Asbury College con-
troller's office to supplement their income.

None of us here at home were aware of the seri-
ousness of their financial crunch. But it was really
beginning to get to Paul. How strange, yet how
lovely it was of God to impress on family and
friends some 3,000 miles away—without one word
from Paul and Marilyn—that we should help them
financially.

One friend, on her way to work, said she "just
knew" she should send $50. Later that night, with-
out mentioning the amount, she suggested the idea
to her husband. His immediate response was, "Yes,
let's do it, and I think we should send $50."

God spoke to several people that week. Each check was sent through Paul's church, and none of the contributors knew about the others. Marilyn said of that time just before the check arrived, "It was Paul's most discouraging and depressing week because of what seemed to be an endless financial struggle."

Since problems never seem to arrive in a stately, orderly way, but in waves (or at least in groups of three), some enormous problems with Marilyn's health were yet to come.

Right in the middle of their scramble for tuition and living expenses, Marilyn became sick. In the days to follow she went from sick to very ill in an alarming manner.

But even in illness the Lord was leading. He put Marilyn's physical care into the very capable hands of Dr. Phyllis Corbitt, a Christian doctor specializing in internal medicine. Doctor Corbitt prayerfully and diligently began her search for the root problem of Marilyn's illness.

As Marilyn's brief journal reads:

Second week: still sick, but I don't know what is wrong.

Today: went to see Dr. C. She found a cyst on one of my ovaries. Also sent in a pregnancy test to lab because I think I may be pregnant.

Pregnancy test came back—negative. Dr. C. is concerned and has scheduled barium enema X ray tests as she thinks there is a blockage in my intestines.

X rays came back neg. Everything was OK. Dr. C. wants me to come into the office Monday.

Monday: Dr. C. found an infection in the uterus. She was just going to prescribe something for it when she stopped and said she had a feel-

ing I just might be pregnant. She took a second
pregnancy test and sent it to another lab.

Tuesday: a nurse called. I *am* pregnant. I'm
going to call Joyce.

Her phone call shook me to my core. She had
been pregnant at the time of the tests, so it meant
the six- to eight-week-old fetus within her had
been X rayed, and the risks and complications involved were pretty overwhelming. Because of possible physical deformation or mental retardation,
Marilyn was facing the decision of keeping the
baby or having an abortion.

*I have heard terrible stories about X ray compli-
cations in the early months of pregnancies. I'm
wondering why she didn't have an abortion immediately—especially in view of the risk.*

If you made a list of all the mothers-to-be in the
whole world, starting at the top with those who
would seek an abortion, Marilyn's name would be
on the bottom of the list. Her spirit is so gentle she
has trouble convincingly swatting a fly into oblivion.

So she decided to keep the baby?

Yes, but not right then.

*From all your writing about her, I sense she is
very close to the Lord. During this time did the
Lord give her a real clear-cut answer immediately,
or did she just grow into her decision? I guess what
I really want to know is this: did she panic? I think
I would have if I'd been faced with that choice.*

Because Marilyn, like the rest of us, has not yet

received sainthood or a glorified body, the sharp edge of panic was in her voice when she talked to me over the phone that day.

If we are at all honest with ourselves, we have to remember that our humanness will have its times of panic. To deny this fact is to lie in the face of reality. Jesus did not eliminate panic when He saved us. We all panic to a certain degree, and until we exchange this corruptible body for a new one, we *will* panic. It is not wrong, or a sin, to panic. It *is* sin to stay in a state of panic. I knew Marilyn well enough to know her stay in "panics-ville" would be real enough, but because of her childlike faith, her anxiety would be short-lived.

What advice did you give her when you talked with her?

I gave her very little advice. The huge decision she was being asked to make had to be answered by the Lord and her own heart.

What were your feelings?

I was in a state of shock and my heart was just breaking for her. It was most difficult for me to realize God really was in control. I'm sure at this point Marilyn had a lot more faith and trust going for her than I did.

I knew that she was going to face pressure in *favor* of an abortion, and that family and friends would pray for a miscarriage. In the weeks to follow she dealt with the pressure as it became a real issue. I did not want to add any stress to her already agonizing decision, so I did not advise either way.

God was so good at this point. He clearly led me to tell her two things. First, I suggested that she get as many professional opinions as she could from other doctors on the risks and problems she faced. Second, I told her that God could very easily work through her doctors, and I promised to pray that God would help her follow their advice—even if it were not what she wanted to hear.

It was at this point in our phone conversation that Marilyn said, "It looks as though I have three options. One, the baby may abort itself, and I'll miscarry. In that case, I will accept it as God's will and God's plan for this pregnancy. Two, the baby may be born with a physical deformity or mental retardation of some degree. If it is, I know God will supply the tremendous grace and love I'll need. Then, with God's help, I will try to be the very best mother in the world. Third, the baby may be born perfectly normal and healthy, and for that miraculous gift I'll be the very best mother God will allow me to be."

Very thoughtfully, she added, "I've no right to accept only the last option as God's will for me, and to reject the others."

She continued our conversation by telling me that she had just read the 91st Psalm. The first verse had a special message for her: "He that dwelleth in the secret place of the most High shall abide under the shadow of the Almighty." Marilyn realized that her baby, in its secret place, could have been protected by the shadow of the Almighty. Then she told me about the fourth verse and said, "Oh, Joyce, I'm just sure God could have covered our baby 'with His feathers' and formed a shield which would have protected the baby from all harmful X rays."

She also read Psalm 139:13–15, and one line in particular took on a new hope-giving significance: "Thou hast covered me in my mother's womb" (v. 13). I'm sure the psalms did for Marilyn what they have been doing for thousands of years—they brought the peace of God surely and deeply into the innermost depths of Marilyn's soul and transformed uncontrolled panic into quiet concern.

It's been a long time since I've really read Psalm 91. Maybe I should reread it.

Yes, definitely. And you should read these verses in every translation available. I feel they are perfect for the expectant mother. David probably didn't mean it that way, but he writes that no evil shall befall thee, no plague shall come near thy dwelling, and that the Lord will give His angels charge over thee. So I feel the message for the about-to-be mother is beautifully clear. At least I'm sure Marilyn felt David wrote the 91st and 139th Psalms just for her, and she delighted in those chapters for all the months of her pregnancy.

Long after her phone call that day, I wept and prayed for her. Marilyn's genuine trust in God's ways is very rare and I prayed and hoped God would notice just how rare.

After Marilyn's next appointment with Dr. Corbitt, the sequence of events was as follows. Here is Marilyn's account:

> Dr. C. had me go to the office today for consultation regarding keeping the baby or having an abortion. She told me she and her staff were praying for us. Also, she is talking with other professionals for opinions.
>
> P.M. I am so confused as to whether or not

I should keep the baby. I can't sleep or stop crying.

I must tell you here that Paul was out of town this night on a speaking engagement for a youth camp, and I'm sure his absence only added to her stress. So there she was, trying to accept the three options, alone, crying, and needing some more direction and leading. She told me later that she had felt as if God were off on the sidelines somewhere watching her struggling with the issues.

Finally, late that night, she said, "Lord, I can't do anything about this situation. I desperately need Your help in deciding which way to go."

Then, slowly but sweetly, the Lord's presence began to engulf her quietly. He seemed to say, "Marilyn, you are going to hear many different opinions as to whether you should keep the baby or not, but I know the final outcome and I want you to simply trust Me."

She got up, washed her face, dried her tears, and—still with a burdened heart—went to bed. She fell instantly asleep, though, and slept the night straight through. It was her first solid sleep in weeks.

When she arrived at work the next morning, she shared her entire predicament with Dr. Eddy, the admissions counselor. Though he was a busy man, he made the time to listen thoughtfully to Marilyn's whole story, and then they prayed together.

It was there, in Dr. Eddy's office, during prayer that Marilyn knew for sure she would keep the baby. That very afternoon several specialists' reports came in, and they all said she should *keep the baby*. In view of the advice the specialists had given me on the West Coast, I could hardly believe the decision of Marilyn's doctors. It was beautiful to see that their conclusion was in step with her God-given direction, and Marilyn's peace was intense.

Paul came home to find that Marilyn had made her choice without him, and God gave him, too, an unexplainable peace about the decision.

Later, in a letter, Marilyn wrote about her prayer life at that time. "I learned from Mother's death I cannot demand anything from God. I'll pray for a healthy baby, but I'll pray knowing He will give me the baby of His choosing."

Oh, but, I'm not sure I could pray in such a liberated way. That's sort of scary, isn't it?

Yes, but that's praying in true freedom because of Christ's love. It's praying realistically for God's best while realizing God's best may not be the "best" in our eyes. It's also praying by trusting with a generous portion of *faith* thrown in.

Marilyn and Paul were putting their blind, obedient, trusting faith in our Lord at a time when they could see no light at the end of the tunnel.

The older I get the more aware I am that *obedience* always precedes peace, holiness, and freedom. It seems that obedience comes first, and then these other things follow; never the other way around.

In the next months of Marilyn's pregnancy I confess I prayed daily, "O Lord, reward this rare kind of obedience of hers with seven or eight months of miracles and a healthy baby."

Did He?

Most definitely. In little ways and big ways

Marilyn and Paul both saw and felt the hands of God.

Those months of pregnancy they were more pressured financially than ever before, but God worked.

Out of the blue a woman gave Marilyn $17 for material to make herself some maternity clothes.

At that same time, Marilyn wrote, "Neat things have been happening to us. My piano teacher told me that she decided to give me lessons—*free* of charge. She said she just felt led to do so and she even came to my office to tell me so."

Then there was that week I described earlier, when the large contribution came from the church.

The day after it came, Marilyn and Paul ate their sack lunches in Marilyn's office. They used her adding machine to figure out how they would spend the money.

As they tallied it all up, they found they could pay off all their present bills except $100 on Paul's book bill.

"Wouldn't it be nice, Paul, if the Lord gave us exactly $100 for that bill?" Marilyn said, quietly. Paul told her not to worry and then said that even though they didn't have it right then, God would work it out and provide it somehow.

His faith was in the expansion business and his spiritual growth was just magnificent.

Later that day Paul returned to pick Marilyn up from the office. As she got into the car Paul said, "You're not going to believe this! I checked our mailbox and there was a receipt in it for $100. I went to the business office to find out about it, and guess what! They told me someone paid the last $100 on my books—anonymously!"

Marilyn wrote, "We don't know who our anonymous benefactor is, and we never told anyone about the bill, but it's paid! How we praise the Lord for the many kindnesses He extends to us! Even though we don't deserve it, He takes care of us."

What about the baby? Has Marilyn delivered yet?

Almost six weeks ago, after only an hour or two of light labor, Marilyn gave birth to a healthy, normal little girl, who looks like a miniature angel without wings and is named Christy Joy.

Marilyn handmade 50 birth announcements (necessity, the mother of invention, again). On them she quoted Hannah's statement of loving obedience about her child Samuel:

> "For this child I prayed; and the Lord hath given me my petition which I asked of Him. Therefore also I have lent him to the Lord, as long as he liveth he shall be lent to the Lord" (1 Sam. 1:27–28).

Hannah asked for that child, but she held him with open arms and never lost sight of the fact he was on a loan from God to be loaned back to God. What obedience!

How very beautiful. I'm so glad God gave Marilyn a healthy baby. I hope mine is healthy, too.

I pray your baby is healthy and normal, too. But don't miss something very important here.

What's that?

It's perfectly possible to give birth to a healthy baby only to have him grow into an active three-year-old, run out into the street, and be taken by

death. We have to hold our children lightly as
Hannah did because they are loaned gifts from
God. Also, I want you to remember this. Had
Marilyn and Paul *not* been given the third option,
the healthy baby, they still would have accepted
the baby and her circumstances with obedient joy.
They still would have sent out the same verse on
their birth announcement, and their dedication to
being the parents the Lord wanted them to be still
would have been just as strong as it is now. They
were *prepared* to take the baby as God's gift to
them regardless of circumstances.

Marilyn said her first thoughts when the nurse
put little Christy Joy in her arms were, "Oh, dear,
I *could* have done away with her. . . ."

Being obedient to God's leading may be the most
difficult thing about being in a corner, but God's
ways are so open and so unlimited that we must
trust Him and His judgments no matter which way
they take us!

*I don't know if I would have the strength and
power to carry through with God's plan as Marilyn
and Paul did.*

Oh, Honey, God gave them the strength, power,
and energy to accept His will only *after* they decided to obey His leading. First they chose to follow and accept; then the Holy Spirit enabled them
to be strong.

St. Paul tells us clearly in Romans 7 that we
stand between two conflicting forces every day of
our lives. On one side are the satanic forces of
evil and sin, and on the other the forces of Jesus
Christ and the righteous. With the sunrise every
morning, we have to make the choice or, better

yet, vote, for the side which will rule the whole day.

When we recognize our corner as God's unlimited corner and *choose* to obey Him, He leads us into the victorious eighth chapter of Romans, and we *shout* with Paul, starting with Romans 8:1, "There is therefore now no condemnation to them which are in Christ Jesus, who walk not after the flesh but after the Spirit." We *choose* to walk in the Spirit and then we read Romans 8:35, "Who shall separate us from the love of Christ? Shall tribulation, or distress, or persecution, or famine, or nakedness, or peril or sword?" Romans 8:37–39 answers the question by saying,

"Nay, in all these things we are more than conquerors through Him that loved us. For I am persuaded, that neither death, nor life, nor angels, nor principalities, nor powers, nor things present, nor things to come, nor height, nor depth, nor any other creature, shall be able to separate us from the love of God, which is in Christ Jesus our Lord."

Wherever we are—even in an *unlimited corner*—we know we can trust God!

Marilyn and Paul have weathered the first of many unlimited corner experiences, and I feel they are on the right track.

Marilyn wrote a thank you note for a baby gift to a friend of ours. It said, "How we praise the Lord for our little daughter! Our prayer now is that we will be the parents God has in mind for us to be and that as parents we will make it easy for Christy Joy to come to know Jesus."

You see, she's starting parenthood now, and believe me . . . there's an unlimited corner if I ever saw one!

10

Used or Usable

*I'm in my late fifties and very discouraged about
the way I look. I'd like to have a face lift or some
cosmetic surgery done, but some of my friends
think a Christian woman shouldn't be so vain. Is
it wrong to want to look younger and better?*

Of course it's not wrong to want to look younger
or better, but I hear you hurting in a different direction from your words, and I wonder if *you'd*
be happy with the results of cosmetic surgery.

*Oh, I'm sure I would. It would mean a new
lease on life for me to look 10 years younger. Who
knows, my husband might even pay a little attention to me for a change.*

He might at that, but *not* because of the surgery.
You would be viewing your own self differently
and that would be the change he'd most likely
notice.

Are you saying a face lift is not the issue here?

That's right. I think you're hurting as a 50-plus woman because of some special fears you're living with right now.

Like what?

Like the fearful feeling that you're all used up and not good for anything anymore, or the fear of retirement, of growing older, or of physically aging with wrinkles, fat, and lagging muscle tone. All these fears are crowding you, aren't they?

Yes, I guess they are. I don't want to become a shapeless, toothless, senile old lady. Yet every day my mirror tells me I'm headed in that direction.

I think you're rushing into the shapeless, toothless, senile bit a little too soon. You are unnecessarily worrying about a bridge you aren't going to cross for a few more years.

But it's such a crime to grow old or, worse, look old.

That's very true in a society that preaches youth and beauty in every corner. In an advertisement the other day, I read the caption, "Do you want to look younger than your daughter?" The answer was, "Yes, of course I do!"

I don't see any "enormous joys" in being old— only the aches and pains of aging. And I'm upset by the looks of pity that young people give me sometimes.

Today I reread the description of the marvelous

model woman in Proverbs 31:25, and I was struck once more with a delicate truth. The first part of the verse says, "Strength and honor are her clothing." Picture this woman now in your mind's eye. The writer has done a remarkable thing here by taking inward qualities and using them as outward adornments in this short sentence. So what does she look like? Can you tell me how old she is? And, better still, does she look used or usable to you?

She looks majestic or regal in my mind's eye, and it's hard to tell if she's over 40 or under.

Majestic or regal? That's very good, and it's just about the same description I'd give if I were asked the same question.

You see, whenever we are right with God, involved in doing His will and not our own, we are clothed in *His strength* and *His honor.*

God's strength and honor inside us are so brilliant that they give our faces and whole countenances quite a soul lift. It's an "inside job" done by the Master Designer Himself.

When I listened to your first statement, I heard a lot of dissatisfaction. I heard very little self-esteem or self-worth, and I suspect you have lost or forgotten your God-given gifts of strength and honor.

Perhaps I have. But maybe it's just that I don't like growing old.

But growing old and the whole aging process is inevitable and—make no mistake about this—it *does* happen to every one of us. Whether we deeply resent it, fight it, or accept it depends directly on us and our attitude.

Are you saying you're against having a face lift and that I should simply accept aging?

No, I'm not against having a face lift, and I don't believe Christian women who have cosmetic surgery are vain. I simply want you to take a better, more balanced look at yourself, and then decide your needs. You may desperately need surgery, but what kind, and by what doctor?

Many a woman has looked into the mirror, seen the wrinkles, lines, and sagging jowls, and has rushed into plastic surgery. She's *sure* it is the answer to her problems in relating to younger people or her children; it's the answer to feeling happy every morning; and it's the answer to bringing romance back into a dying marriage.

After the surgery has been completed and has healed, she looks into the mirror and sees a delightful 10-years-fresher face on the same old body with the same old problems raging inside, and her frustration knows no limits.

Back to the lady in Proverbs. After we are told what she wears as clothing, the verse continues, "And she shall rejoice in time to come." It seems to me that since she knows where her strength, honor, and general dignity originate, she may look to the future (the "time to come") and be joyously happy about aging.

Here are some other translations of this verse:

"She dresses in strength and nobility; and she smiles at the future" (AAT).

"Strength and dignity are her clothing, and she smiles at the future" (NASB).

But my favorite is:

"She is a woman of strength and dignity, and has no fear of old age" (LB).

I wrote in *To Lib or Not to Lib* (Victor Books, 1972), "If strength and dignity are the words used to describe her, then I think you can safely assume she likes being herself and her age. She had enjoyed every stage of her life and the fear of growing old has not tarnished her beauty."

Later I said of my mother, "She didn't grow old inside. She loved every plateau of age she reached and never stopped wanting to learn. Change did not threaten her, it only challenged her. I want to age in that same way."

Tell me, what age are you right now, exactly?

Fifty-seven and holding.

I love your sense of humor, but you *do know* you're *not* holding, don't you? Every year at our birthday we have a brand new 365 days, Lord willing, to be the persons God wants us to be.

Think of this! We have a whole new year to gain some knowledge, to expand in wisdom, to change some bad habit, or to learn from last year's mistakes! Each year doesn't need to threaten us; it can present a challenge. However, none of us is *holding* at any age, nor is holding right, or even God's plan.

I'm 44 at this writing, and I am looking forward to being 45 next February. It will be a new opportunity *not* to make the same mistakes, *not* to open my mouth out of season, and *not* to repeat this year's boo-boos! It's a whole new year, and while I'm showing all the signs of physical aging, I'm also one year more matured (hopefully) and one year more advanced in caring, sharing, and loving. I don't want to miss the *nows* of life by wishing for the good ol' days of my youth, or by fantasying about the future's plans and picnics.

God has put us here in our own time and at our own ages, and I long to see Christian women *rejoice* in whatever age they are.

I'm getting your message, but I'm about 13 years older than you, and things are falling apart a bit faster at this stage of the ball game.

That's true, but you just reminded me of the little 80-plus-year-old lady who gave the latest results from her physical by reporting that "Everything is just in perfect condition." Then with her eyes twinkling, she added confidentially, "But, you know, it's my mind I miss."

I guess I need to look at the aging process with a little more humor because, as you said, it does hit everybody. However, one thing you said at the beginning about my fear is accurate. You talked of my fearful feeling that I was "all used up." As I realize now, that is a very real fear. How can I cope with the feelings of uselessness I'm beginning to have?

Let me tell you about Helen Gunn—Mrs. Harvey Gunn—but to thousands of people, just plain old Mrs. Gunn.

She has been in our church for 1,002 years, or at least it seems that way. She and Mr. Gunn were to the junior high department what the giant pillars holding up the roof of our church are: solid strength, dependable, and *always* there.

Our daughter and son, like thousands of other

kids, remember the Gunns as "indefatigable, unde-
featable, and unbeatable." They outlasted the kids
at any beach party or church function. There
never seemed to be anything that stopped them . . .
except that a few years ago Mr. Gunn did an un-
thinkable thing. He died and went home to be with
the Lord.

Being a widow was hard on Mrs. Gunn. She was
lonely, I'm sure, but it didn't seem to stop her or
even slow her down. She continued her work pace
and was continually used of God.

But all that changed just a few weeks ago.

Now 84 years old, she suffered a series of strokes.
Since her doctor felt she must not be left alone, it
appeared that Mrs. Gunn would live the rest of her
days in a local convalescent home.

My secretary, Sheila, was one of those junior high
kids of past years, and she had kept up her friendship with the Gunns. Sheila was badly shaken
when she returned from her first visit to the convalescent home. All she could think of was Mrs.
Gunn's new "home": a bed, a tiny shelf, and a
closet for her belongings in a three-bed hospital-
type ward with a flimsy curtain to draw around
her bed for privacy.

During her next visit, Sheila commented on the
sweet, uncomplaining spirit with which Mrs. Gunn
had accepted this sudden turn of events, noting
what a trauma it must have been to leave the home
she had lived in all those years with her children
and dear Mr. Gunn, how hard it must have been
to leave her keepsakes and her neighbors, and how
difficult it must be for her to lie on that bed and
picture her beautiful rose garden now in full bloom.

Mrs. Gunn's response was so classic, I'm sure it
was entered immediately in God's record books in

heaven for all of us to read when we get there. She said, "Well, many years ago I told the Lord I'd go wherever He wanted me to go and do whatever He wanted me to do. It looks like this is where He wants me."

Then she added, "I'm anxious to see how God will use me in my failing years. I can't get out any more, so it will have to be with those who come to me."

If I didn't know it before, I know it now for sure: Mrs. Helen Gunn is a real, live saint of God.

At 84 this woman is not all used up, washed up, or wrung out, but is a vibrant woman who is *usable* beyond belief and is alive with God.

In comparison with your Mrs. Gunn, my feelings of being old and used up are rather ridiculous, aren't they?

You said that—I didn't—but I'm glad you have seen a different perspective on aging. Mrs. Gunn is almost 30 years older than you, but she's not missing one single second of the *nows* God has planned for her.

I don't know how many days, weeks, or years she has left here on earth, but her remarks to Sheila have added a dimension to my life in learning.

At 44 I've learned a real truth in all of this. Mrs. Gunn has been laid on the shelf, so to speak, but she is willing to be usable, and that makes all the difference. She's not demanding to be used, but rather, is open to being usable and simply eager to see how God will accomplish this purpose now that she's confined.

Your shelf holds fears of growing old, but it

could hold babies and diapers, or an alcoholic husband, or any number of circumstances. If you're not willing to be usable—right on that shelf—God will never use you next door, in the next town, or the next country.

Thank you for zeroing-in on my real inner conflicts and problems. I'm going to give my mind and heart to some in-depth prayer time over this whole question of aging and face lifts.

Actually, the decision to have cosmetic surgery is strictly up to you. Cosmetic surgery is available not only for face lifts but also for little boys' ears which stick out and are the object of teasing, or for a large, overwhelming nose. It's easy to arrange, but the decision for you to make is a personal one and should be made after much prayer and soul searching.

I would hate for you to put all kinds of hope into cosmetic surgery only to find the inner problems still there after the outer surgery has healed.

I would hate, even more, for you to miss all of God's *now* plans for you while you're in your fifties, sixties, and seventies!

Happy birthday next February, Joyce!

Thanks!

11

Fourteen
and Feeling Awful

I'm 14 and I feel just awful. I used to really like my parents, but now all they do is bug me. It's really getting to me. I just don't know what's going on anymore. Am I the only one who feels this way, or does this happen to all teenagers?

It certainly does, and you're right on schedule! Any time after you're about 12 years of age a little voice deep down inside of you whispers, "You're not a baby any more and you're sure no adult. You're just a 'never-gonna-make-it' kid." And for the next few years, depending on how well you listen to that voice, the only word for your feelings is *awful*. In fact, if I asked you to describe yourself with one word, what would you choose?

Ugly.

That's just wild! Do you know that every time

I've asked that of a 14-, 15-, or 16-year-old I've gotten *exactly* the same answer?

I guess that's because we are ugly.

Well, maybe you think you are, but all of us are ugly in different ways.

Even adults?

Especially adults. There are lots of different kinds of "uglies" around. The physical ugly is only one. There's the mentally mixed-up or disturbed ugly, and certainly the emotional ugly, and some people even suffer from the spiritual uglies.

How long am I going to feel this way?

Honey, I don't know how long it will be for you. Some kids have a defiant spirit and stay in it for a long time. Others have a compliant spirit and the time is relatively short. How long you feel ugly and awful depends on things like temperament, circumstances of family life, and especially your relationship with the Lord.

I only wish this time of life did not come as such a surprise to teenagers. I wish, even more, every parent could take Dr. James Dobson's fantastic suggestions about handling problems of adolescence and listen to his excellent tapes, "Preparing for Adolescence" (One Way and Vision House publishers) on the subject of pre-teens and teenagers.

Why is that?

Well, it's just because he is so right-on about

kids. For instance, he suggests parents sit down with their child when he or she is about 10 years old, and outline on a sheet of paper some of the things which will happen during the teen years. (Like the fact you will probably not care too much for your parents, your mother's choice of clothes, your frustrating sexual development, your present family life-style or your fluctuating spiritual values.) The parents should make this long list, explaining that these things are only temporary, and then the list should be stored in a drawer until its predictions start coming true.

That way when you are 14 and can't stand your 40-plus mother or dad, at least you and your folks can look up the list and remember you knew it would be this way, and you eliminate the "surprise" of this awful feeling.

When both our kids were in the teen years, all of us repeated a saying which, to this day, makes us smile, but which is so true: "This too shall pass!" And we said it nearly every day. It helped a little.

Well, my mom didn't write a list like that or talk with me so what do we do now?

Try and have the talk now.

Are you kidding? We start to talk and it just ends up one big yelling match.

That's probably because your timing's off a little. Sometimes we try to iron out conflicts and rules when we are in the heat of rushing and scheduling. Avoid that like a plague! Talk to your mom when dinner is *not* being made, or company coming, or when your mom's in the middle of trying to get a sleeve sewn in, because nobody is able to talk in a rational way when there's pressure or stress around.

When you do get a chance to talk, try to keep an open mind about the problems. If you've decided you *know* what your mom is going to say, then you are just as bad as the parents who never let their kids finish a sentence, and you know how frustrating that is. Don't talk about the people so much as the problem. We get into all kinds of trouble when we say, "You *always* let Jim do that, but you don't like me, so you *never* let me do it." That's going after the people and not the problem.

How do I state that question, then?

By saying, "I'd like to do such and such. You haven't let me before, but could I now?" If the answer is no, then say, "I'd like to know your thinking and reasons." Then, remember, if your mind is open, you may hear something that *does* make sense.

Yes, but what if my parents' minds are closed?

They might have good reason from past experiences. Their attitude may be wrong, but who said parents are perfect?

In defense of your folks, I have to say that you get only one shot at being parents, and it is extremely tough to get through parenthood without making a few mistakes and unpleasant memories. Try to catch the significant concept that your mom and dad are no *superparents*. They are real people with real hang-ups just like you.

Your mom has down days when everything boggles her mind just like some of your days. Your dad can get so caught up in the mechanics of working, moonlighting, making a living, that his "home" time is rare, and he may have little talent for communication.

What separates you from your parents is some years. You are not a baby, but you haven't the years it takes to make an adult. On the other hand, you're on the edge of being an adult.

You are pressured by parents, peer groups, teachers, and society as a whole. Your parents are pressured by the same things. The only difference is that your parents have been pressured longer by outside influences and, in most cases, they seem to be able to take it in their stride a little better.

It is important to have friends, to be well-liked, and we all care about being loved (no matter how much we deny it). But don't make these concerns the goal of your every waking hour.

But my friends are important.

I agree. But as a mother, I have to say there are times when other things pre-empt friends, wishes, or rules. I remember that Laurie wouldn't dream of wearing anything her friends would not wear. But when she wanted to wear short, short hot-pants to Sunday School I said no. It nearly broke her heart because "Everybody is wearing them," she wailed. I didn't let her wear hot pants for the same reason I wouldn't let her wear a velvet formal into the swimming pool next door. (I wouldn't care if everyone were swimming in formals or not; it simply would not be the becoming, practical, or right thing to wear swimming.) She was mad for weeks, but now that she is almost 21 and is choosing her own clothes, I see our old-fashioned training has paid off. She dresses in the best of taste, using the soft summer colors which look marvelous with her blonde hair and denim-blue eyes, and she is a trend-setter instead of being a trend-follower.

That must be nice. I don't think I'll ever be 21.

Oh, Honey, you will. It only *feels* as though time has stopped. Actually, it's moving right along and the days of feeling like a fish out of water, of not being able to like your present situations, will ease. Believe me, they will ease!

But, meanwhile, be careful about choosing friends. Paul talks about our responsibility to have the right friends. Just listen to this: "What I meant was that you are not to keep company with anyone who claims to be a brother Christian but indulges in sexual sins, or is greedy, or is a swindler, or worships idols, or is a drunkard, or abusive. Don't even eat lunch with such a person" (1 Cor. 5:11, LB). Follow that verse with this powerful one: "I can do anything I want to if Christ has not said no, but some of these things aren't good for me. Even if I am allowed to do them, I'll refuse to if I think they might get such a grip on me that I can't stop when I want to" (1 Cor. 6:12, LB).

If you were my mother, what would you want me to be like?

That's the most iffy question I've ever been asked, but I hear you asking for some guidelines of a sort. Is that it?

Yes, I guess I'd like to know what you'd expect from me.

All right, here are some things which may help you at 14 with those "awful" feelings, but this list is not a "cure-all" or a pat-answer list for everything in your life right now. I'm assuming that you are a Christian, so I'll take it from there.

1. *Try to remember this age is hard on the others in the family, too.* They are all adjusting to the changes which come with the teen years— just as you are. So ask the Lord to help you be still on some matters, patient on others, and willing to accept the blame when it really is your fault. It's all part of growing up.

2. *Keep in mind none of us gets everything he wants.* During the teen years you will want more of everything, from new clothes to new ideas. Idealistically, spiritually, and even materialistically, you will search and feel the need for expanding and growing. But don't be too hard on yourself when some things are not easily available. *Everything* takes time.

3. *Try wearing your parents' shoes.* Try to understand your working mother, your tense dad, your parents' financial crunch. Being sensitive to some of *their* fears will ease a lot of inner tension within you, not to mention around the house.

Paul tells us to forgive others as God through Christ forgave us (Eph. 4:32). That's really heavy, but once you get the idea, it's incredible what God can do with attitudes. Try forgiving your mom for being 40, or your dad for being preoccupied. It's an exercise in real Christian living.

Sometimes teenagers are so totally involved in what to wear, where to go, and who's going to be there, they lose sight of anyone else's plans or problems. You kinda get tunnel vision. So watch for it, and try to open your field of visual perception a little wider. Forgiving your parents for being the way they are is a giant step in the right direction.

4. *Once in a while say, "I think you're right, Mom. I hadn't thought of it that way"—and mean it.* The wise teenager doesn't try to outwit others and win every argument. Life is made up of giving and taking. There are times when it's best to take it and other times when it's best to give in. These sentences are good sentences to learn right now, for your adult-on-your-own life later.

We are told in the Scriptures to honor our parents, and that if we do so as a conscious act of the will, we will have less trouble respecting all other authority in the adult world later on (Eph. 6:1–4).

5. *Take a solemn vow to show an act of kindness to both Mom and Dad each day.* They will probably go into immediate shock or cardiac arrest, but they'll revive. A kind word, a thank you, or a pat on the back from a teenager is very rare, but it produces miraculous changes in adults— especially parents. Keep this verse in mind: "And whatever you do, do it with kindness and love" (1 Cor. 16:14, LB).

Yesterday a note from Laurie said,

Bye Mom,

I hope your time today at Dr. Borland's [the dentist who is doing a lot of work on my jaw] goes okay.

You amaze me in your attitude because by now, after all these months, I'd be ready to be the world's greatest complainer.

I love you and I missed being with you yesterday. Have a good day.

Love always,
Laurie

Writing this note was an act of kindness that took only a minute or two from her fast pace of getting ready for school, but she restored my soul. Acts like this make it fairly simple to keep the lines of communication wide open.

6. *Take an even more solemn vow to live a straight, honest life.* You'll find this very hard in the fraudulent times we live in, but the teenager who lies to his parents and family betrays a sense of trust which rarely is reestablished. First you tell one lie, then a few lies to cover the one, and finally you lie to yourself. Then the loser is you. Evidently lying was a real problem to the early Christians. Otherwise the writers of the New Testament would not have given it so much attention. So take heart. We all have to work at honesty. I've noticed it never comes easy—at least it doesn't for me.

7. *Work out agreements about rules before the conflict arises.* It's easier to accept rules and regulations (and we must have them if we are to live with one other person in the same house) when you know them in advance. Rules about dating, use of the phone, getting a car, or time to be in at night all need to be talked out with your folks when you are *not* in the heat of a battle over it. Again—it's a matter of timing. The smart teenager thinks ahead.

8. *Ask for your parents' help and advice from time to time.* There are very few parents in the world who wouldn't respond to a teenager's plea of, "I need your help." Your parents' self-esteem would be strengthened, too, by your asking. (Yes, parents as well as teenagers have real problems in the self-worth department.)

9. *Remember, your parents are not mind readers.*

If something is bothering you, you must be willing to talk and to communicate your need. Too often all a family hears is a bunch of mumbling from a kid who's in a rotten mood. Everybody *knows* something's wrong, but nobody knows *what*. So, level with your parents.

I don't know if my mom will read this or not, but in case she does, what would you tell her?

OK—here again are just some suggestions. They may or may not help, but I pray they do.

1. *Shift gears in your tone of voice, from mother-to-child talk to mother-to-young-adult talk.* It's very hard to realize these children are about to be grown up. We remember the days of their *total* dependency when they were babies, but now we must shift our gears to accommodate the *growth* factor. Talk to your teenagers as people. They are not dependent babies any more, and the struggle of growth between adolescence and adulthood is a very real fear and concern to them. Talking to them on a person-to-person approach reinforces their self-esteem at a time when they desperately need it.

2. *Release new freedoms of choice with every birthday during the teen years.* Each year on their birthday, you may turn over new responsibilities and new privileges to them. It's a way of helping them out the door of childhood and into the world of adulthood, and if it's done every year, turning them loose at 20 will not be such a scary thing for you.

I personally enjoyed sitting down with our kids on their birthdays and saying, "OK, now that you're 16, we are taking off such and such restriction. You set the time limit, or the rule." Each time I did this, I could almost see the kid add another inch to his or her height.

This plan was also helpful when a younger sister came along and said, "How come Rick gets to do such and such?" It's not fair!" We could respond with, "Wait a minute. When you turned 14, we let you do some things you didn't get to do at 12, and when you get to be 16 like Rick, you'll have a whole bunch of new things to try out. So it *is* fair."

3. *Pray with your husband in a solid, united way for this teenager.* Many times I phoned my husband at the bank to sob frantically, "I've had it with Laurie. She's driving me absolutely bananas today. Nothing I do is right. I can't talk to her. I don't know if I can stand her rebellious attitude another second . . ." Then my husband interrupted my 6 o'clock bad news report with, "Dear Jesus, we bring Laurie to you again and we ask You to give us the wisdom we need in dealing with her attitudes . . ." Dick would pray for me, too and ask God to calm me. *Always, always,* God answered my husband's prayer. I'd hang up the phone, take a deep breath, feel the peace of God, and hang in there for another hour or so. You and your husband can have a rich ministry in prayer over your teenagers, and God's hand can work beautifully in your love—not only with the teenager, but with each of you as well.

4. *Pray even harder for your teenager's friends.* While parents, teachers, and many adults lose their influence, the teenager's peers grow in their ability to convince and set attitudes. Friends are very important in the life of a teenager, so it is imperative that you hold the friends up before the Lord in prayer *always.* All your teenager needs is one really

bad friend in order to go down the tubes. On the other hand, all your teenager needs is one really good friend to keep straight. So never stop praying for the friends.

In Rick's junior year of high school, he came home one day and said, "Mom, I don't have any really neat Christian friends." We began to talk about it. I suggested we write out a "project" list of names. Rick wrote down four names of guys he liked. Two of them were not Christians, and the other two were not really too serious about their Christian commitment.

Then our whole family prayed over these four names and in the next year or so we saw all of them either find the Lord, as Mark and Gordon did, or really dedicate their lives to Christ, as Scott and Mike did. To this day, the five young men (and their wives, now) are dear friends in Christ, and God is blessing each life in a unique way.

I'm not a bit modest when I say my husband and I definitely feel that we are a part of these young men's successes, because we prayed daily, and sometimes hourly, for all of them.

5. *Try to give your teenager some undivided attention each week.* One family I know has six children, yet the parents manage to have some *private* together time for each child during the week. The mother said, "It takes enormous planning, but kids are great at putting up with anything, including setbacks and disappointments, if they know they *will* have that special alone time with us." Sometimes the time is not really alone, but special, like taking only one child to do the grocery shopping. They talk and cut-up all the time at the store, and though the mother's attention is a little divided, she manages to get in a lot of communication

with the teenager who walks along beside her.

Try taking a noncommunicative teenager to lunch at McDonald's or a "fun" restaurant, as Laurie and I have done. It does wonders for bridging the communication gap.

6. *If talking doesn't seem to work very well, try the "note approach."* Sometimes teenagers are very unsure of themselves verbally, but on paper they become almost eloquent. Leave love notes, not lectures or critical remarks, in their bedroom, their schoolbooks, or Scotch-Taped to their bathroom mirror. Messages like,

"I know you're worried about that stupid history test today. I'll be really praying for your mind to remember all you've learned," Or,

"The *fact* that your face has a new bunch of skin problems doesn't change the *fact* that you're loved!"

Messages like this may change the course of a teenager's direction, and may well be the very thing which gets him across the channel from adolescence to adulthood with the minimum of bruising and hurts.

7. *Forgive your teenager for being 14.* Earlier in this chapter I talked about Ephesians 4:32. The same words apply to parents. Remember what it was like to be 14? When I ask an audience if they'd like to be 14 again, the answer is a resounding, unanimous no! So it's important that you forgive and accept these 14- (15-, 16-, or 17-) year-old teenagers *where they are.* Don't tell them their fears are silly. Those fears are all too real. Remember some of yours? Don't lecture them in front of their friends. Some parents seem to take an obnoxious delight in embarrassing their children in public. Most of all, forgive them for being the age

they are and erase forever the sentences, "Why don't you grow up? You're acting like a stupid kid!" How else are kids supposed to act, Mom? Hopefully they will mature with age and time, but telling them to grow up is superfluous. They *are* growing up, no matter how slowly, so accept them where they are!

You know, Joyce, you're really a neat lady. Thanks for all you've said. I feel a little less awful now.

Great!

12

Happiness or Joy?

I was really annoyed this morning! I had just gone through the traumatic upheaval of the usual early morning sprint to get my husband off to work, girls off to school, me and baby, plus equipment trunks, off to the church for your meeting when I saw you

I came charging up the steps from the nursery and there you were in the vestibule, talking to the women's missionary chairman. I think at that moment I hated you because there you were . . . smiling, talking, and looking absolutely lovely. Every hair was in place. I reached up to smooth my hair a bit and a green plastic curler fell out. You were wearing a beautiful dark printed velvet suit. It must be nice to wear something and not have baby's lint all over it! And your bow blouse was my favorite shade of peach. You looked so radiant and glowing.

To me, you were the essence of everything I was not. I gave you a scalding look and, of all things, you returned it with a gracious smile and mouthed the words, "Good Morning." I thought, "Sweet Really sweet. How sickening," and then I stomped down the aisle to one of the few seats left.

To myself I fumed, "Lady, if it wasn't for the fact that I promised my friend I'd come—well, I wouldn't have been here on a bet. Especially since I've just seen you. You don't know anything at all about the real live world and all its unfairness. You know nothing of working like mad to keep a marriage not only straight but fun, of adolescence and babies, of grief or growing old. And for the life of me, I can't figure out why I'm here!"

Then, for crying out loud, you began your program by sitting down at the piano. You played one perfect arpeggio up the keyboard and then proceeded to sing "There Is a Quiet Place" as Ralph Carmichael must dream of having it sung. Well, that did it! Your talent was about all I needed to eject me up and out of my seat, but I reconsidered because it would have been awkward to leave. So I stayed.

I'm writing this to tell you I'm really glad I didn't walk out. I would have missed so very much.

Little things really do mean a lot, and as you talked I couldn't believe my ears. First of all, you're 10 years older than I am; you almost committed suicide before you became a Christian; you work daily at your marriage; you are a mother and a mother-in-love; death took a baby son, a grandfather, and your mother all within a short time. So you know, really know, a good deal about life and its injustices and stress. Yet you still managed to look like happiness itself.

I guess I'm really writing because I need to ask your forgiveness for my TV-type, instant-replay, judgmental opinion of you. But I also want to ask you why my attitude was so "set" and so off base You seemed so together and, yes, so very *happy and serene. Why did I resent you so much?*

I love your letter because every time I speak there are always several people like you in the audience. Your letter reads like a favorite and familiar book to me. I've certainly heard these comments before, and you are by no means alone in your "instant" assessment. Besides, you probably reacted on a tummy that had no breakfast, and that condition tends to add all sorts of complications to our feelings about people and situations.

Let me talk about your line, "You seemed so together and, yes, so very happy."

Anyone, and I do mean *anyone*, can manage, at least for short periods of time, to manufacture the "look of being together and happy." We do it all the time. We wear "together and happy" masks, especially when we are in public, when others will probably observe us. I don't believe there's any trick to "looking happy." In fact, *you* could have done it in spite of your hectic morning track record. You could have merely set a dial in your mind to "happy" and pulled it off pretty well. Women are excellent actresses. The problem is, it's only a skin-deep look, and given any time or stress, it vanishes.

I know, now, that you hadn't pushed the "happy-look" button for the big "together put-on." But what did I see?

I'm not trying to sound like a saint, but what you sensed—rather than saw—was a thing called joy. A thing that has *nothing* to do with happiness—nothing whatsoever—yet often people confuse the two.

I wish I'd kept track of all the times people have written or talked with me about getting happiness, having happiness, or finding happiness.

I simply do not find, in any of the Bible's translations, the implication that as Christians we will discover the kind of blissful, never ending, uninterrupted, extraordinary happiness we seek.

I guess I'd better find out what the difference is, then, between happiness and joy.

Great! I thought you'd never ask! There is an incredible difference between them, especially for the Christian. The sad thing I see is this: There are Christians who spend just as much energy wishing, praying, and working toward achieving happiness as non-Christians, when what they should be looking for is joy.

I looked up the word *happiness* in several dictionaries. What says it best is a huge, out-of-print dictionary/encyclopedia published in 1911. It describes happiness as "the state of being happy and the pleasurable experience that springs from possessions of good, the gratification of the desires, or relief from pain or evil; enjoyment; as, one's *happiness* depends on oneself."

In other words, happiness depends on our circumstances. Other dictionaries state that the word *happiness* comes from *happenchance*. My trusty old dictionary goes on to say, "Happy originally refers to something that comes 'by good hap'—a *chance* that brings prosperity, benefit, or success."

So in order for me to be happy or have happiness, the circumstances around me *must* be in apple-pie order.

I am happy at this moment because it's spring,

because my sister, Marilyn, gave birth to a healthy baby girl, because my children love me, because my husband made me feel loved tonight, because I talked with my friend Clare, and because today was a day of minimal pain. Because of these events and circumstances, I had a "happy day" as the saying goes.

Joy, on the other hand, is not dependent on anything that happens outside my body—neither by happenchance nor circumstance. It has everything to do with an inner happening.

Back to my old dictionary. It says, "Joy is more intense than happiness, deeper than gladness, to which it is akin, but nobler and more enduring than pleasure."

Joy is more, more, and more! Joy grows deep within me, involving my development and growth with God. Technically, as I grow older, this joy should mature and become even stronger. I believe the "mean-old-lady" syndrome should never develop in the Christian senior citizen. (Now that I've said this, I'm sure my family is going to watch me closely as I age to see if my joy matures or I become a crotchety old lady!)

Paul tells us that when the Holy Spirit is in control of our lives, He will produce what is called the fruit of the Spirit (Gal. 5:22). Wouldn't you know, second on the list, after love, is joy. It should be a product of our lives.

Happiness is transient, easily upset, quickly lost, and completely dependent on what's going on around us. In contrast, *joy* knows no such limitations. It does not come and go or rise and fall like a kite at the end of a string or a chancy, windy day.

What really tickled me about your letter was

your confirmation that I'm right in my evaluation of happiness and joy. Actually, the morning at the meeting was quite different for me from the way you saw it.

I am glad you didn't notice the red burn on my right hand. I got popped by hot oil when I was frying tacos the day before. Or the blister which split open each time someone shook my hand. I'm pleased you didn't catch any of the pain from my aching jaw, which was really beginning to hassle me. You couldn't have known, of course, but the carpets outside my motel room were shampooed from midnight to 2 A.M. that morning, and I felt as though I'd been up all night with a colicky baby. I'm grateful you didn't see the dark purple circles under my eyes, carefully camouflaged with an extra dab of makeup. My heart is warmed that you didn't guess I was concerned and praying for a political science exam Laurie was taking that day. And about my velvet suit. The day will come when you, too, can wear dark lint-catching suits, but here's my side. I have very little time to shop for clothes, so about two or three times a year I buy a seasonal outfit that is just as smashing as I can find. It becomes my uniform for several months. You saw this winter's uniform with one of two blouses I bought for it, and I had already worn it to three months of meetings, luncheons, and TV interviews. I'm glad you liked it, but truly, I'm a little weary of it. And finally, I was hysterically pleased you didn't suspect I'd eaten something earlier which at that moment was rumbling about my stomach like a grumpy lion, eager to get out of his cage.

You see, I was not too terribly happy that morning. I wasn't putting on a phony front. Had you come right up and asked me how I had slept or how I felt, I would have told you straight out. But the circumstances of the morning could not drown out the voices of joy inside me. It was their song you really heard. Actually, I don't think I could have faked enough happiness to cover all those dreadful circumstances that morning, as I look back on it now.

Why did I resent that look of joy, then, especially since it was genuine?

Because you thought it was carefree happiness. You assumed nothing bad was happening to me while in your life, you had seen your world fly apart in 22 directions that morning. After what you'd been through, you didn't know how anybody could be "cheerful" or "together."

Exactly. It's amazing, but as I've just now begun to look at the difference between happiness and joy, I see I have spent years looking for the wrong thing.

Join the crowd. Our society and our peers tell us to go after happiness. But our Bible says the Holy Spirit will produce joy. We all tend to emphasize the wrong thing from time to time.

It is the *joy* of Christ which wins the unsaved to the Lord. That lovely fruit of the Spirit, joy, is what really makes a non-Christian stop dead in his tracks and say, "Whatever it is you have, I want it too!"

You could say, then, that happiness is a human quality which is dependent on outside happenings, but joy is a superhuman trait dependent on a God-given relationship.

Yes, and you've said it beautifully. One could easily become jealous of a person's radiant joy in the face of life's everyday setbacks, but God has promised to produce joy in our lives if we really let the Holy Spirit have control. However, the fruits of the Spirit will never be produced in us without our obedience to the Lord. Joy seems to come only *after* we obey.

The day you saw me, had I taken matters into my own hands and responded to my own feelings of unhappiness, I would have caught the next flight home. That morning, for me, was just as disastrous as yours, yet both of us did what we felt we should; we came to the meeting and obeyed God.

As we did so, He met the needs of both of us. He gave me joy in spite of everything; and He gave you joy, plus a day of learning and maturing.

This story has been repeated so many times. I find I'm somewhere in the process of obeying the Lord, under dreadful circumstances, and smack dab in the middle I find He is producing inexplicable joy! Funny how that works: We obey; He produces.

Let me finish this conversation by encouraging you to read the next lines very carefully.

"And I pray that Christ will be more and more at home in your hearts, living within you as you trust in Him. May your roots go down deep into the soil of God's marvelous love; and may you be able to feel and understand, as all God's children should, how long, how wide, how deep, and how high His love really is; and to experience this love for yourselves, though it is so great that you will never see the end of it or fully know or understand it. And so at last you will be filled up with God Himself" (Eph. 3:17–19, LB).

What a thought—being "filled up with God Himself." That means we have no need to wish and long for happiness as though it were a pot of gold at the end of some nonexistent rainbow. We are free to stop coveting someone else's talents, looks, or life-style, and we no longer need to carry our knapsack of guilt on our backs—guilt over our inadequate feelings. We can trust our Lord. We can obey Him. We can begin to understand the vast magnitude of His love, and we can *expect* the joy of the Lord to fill us from head to toe!

A supernatural miracle—to be filled up with God Himself: Yes, and the best news of all is that it's available to *all* of us, with a capital *A!*